Wave Makers
Inspired Women Building and Living with No Limits

Co-authored by:

Amie Pouges

Cathy Hageman, LE

Susan Jones

Nicole Lynn

Shea Kramer, DC

Cindy Balsley

Angela Holt

Lisa Stubbs

Lisa Statzer

TABLE OF CONTENTS

In my organizing, I attract a lot of people who work from home, some work for larger companies and get to office from home while others are leaving corporate America to follow their dreams and passions. Work-Life Blend and ways to grow the business and networking always come up. I've always wanted to do some training around those topics, but not the same old way it's already being done. This is where Kimberly Pitts of UImpact stepped in and the Community of Wave Maker's was created with the help of Piper The Flying Pig.

What is a Wave Maker you may ask? A Wave Maker is a woman who is spreading her wings in her home, business, and life. Wave-Makers are Inspiring, have No Limits, are Gracious, & support Success. What does a Flying Pig have to do with any of it? I've always loved the phrase, "If Pig's Could Fly" to me that doesn't mean something isn't going to happen it represents dreams and hopes and thinking BIG!! What is going to resonate with your heart and soul so deeply that a statement like If Pig's Could Fly would have you dig your heels in and make that dream come true?!?!

The ladies represented in this book are true Wave Makers in their businesses and their homes. When you read their stories, you will know why!! I am so proud of them for the vulnerability and transparency they showed in sharing their obstacles, victories, and life lessons. There are no fake FB profiles here. Our hope is that you will discover you are not alone and be encouraged to continue to dream.

Sincerely,
Nicole & Piper
www.AWaveMaker.com

AMIE POUGES
The Melody in the Mess

The juggling act of life is messy and seems to be the most prevalent challenge of the working woman! We have much to do and multiple people depending on us to deliver. There is an increasing "Insta-pot level" pressure building, for us to deliver our ever-demanded services with excellence. People are depending on it, always. We make life happen and do an incredible job of keeping the balls in the air for extended periods of time. We impact others positively when we deliver well, but there comes a time when a ball will drop, and all the disappointments and costs will quickly be counted, most loudly by ourselves. This is where the greatest productivity drain will always be found. We are the most active personal critic and creator of self- shame we will ever encounter. It doesn't have to be this way. There is something beautiful just under the surface, but it takes some intentional awareness, and self-talk adjustments, if we are to appreciate it.

There is a melody in this mess we are traversing. The key to enjoying life is hearing the melody and finding your own personal groove when you do. The mess isn't going anywhere, but that doesn't mean you can't dance your way right through it. There will be failures. There will be negative impacts, disappointments, and unplanned detours. There will also be victories and unexpected laughter during the trials, as they are all interwoven rather than linear points on a timeline. Take a moment to acknowledge even the small wins and laugh every chance you get. It's acceptable to have fun, laugh, and find joy despite the challenges that surround you. Don't wait for all things to be right before you enjoy yourself! There is an abundance of women looking for a way to experience joy during a difficult journey, and you could be an example they need to see and would happily emulate. That's powerful if you think about it. You could assist with changing the tone for the better, in their life. That is an important assist that fits into the natural nurturer mojo you likely already embrace.

To see ourselves as a community of women rather than engaging in competition is the beginning place of peace. I decided not to enter that pageant (I can't tap dance anyway) or put on my boxing gloves to step in a ring with another woman. Why? Because **comparison is the assassin of inspiration and vision**, and we invite it in like a welcomed guest, at every turn. You are uniquely gifted and talented and equipped for what you are called to do. You and I are not the same and that is something to embrace, not to become discouraged by. Home décor and fashion may be second nature to you, while I feel like I am flying into the Bermuda Triangle and the little black box may begin to fail at any moment. I am also not the most organized gal you will find in our band of women, but I have the gift of gab and happen to love people as much as I enjoy chocolate, and that my lady is a bunch! To expect us to be excellent or even interested in the same areas is not only unrealistic, but ridiculous. We are different! That is the single most beautiful aspect of life. We can learn, enjoy, and appreciate what is special in one another, but only when we look through the lens of community and not competition. If we each had the same strengths or were perfect in all ways, that would be boring beyond belief. I enjoy laughing at my flops and having a little fun with myself, and I may giggle in good fun when you mess up too, so long as you are tough enough to handle it! I remember in high school when my BFF got nailed in the face with a volleyball during PE (we were the PE girls, not the athletic, make the team kind of superstars you may imagine), her glasses went flying and I was laughing like a lunatic as I ran to ensure she was okay. She was fine, but never let me forget that I mixed the order up on my response to her face being in the wrong place! Safety check, then laughter, I have it down now. That's the kind of stuff that happens and if you can't laugh your way through it, we may just sit in a corner and cry!

I suggest we walk proudly in our specialty rather than hiding in the shadows of disappointment for what we are lacking. You would be common rather than uniquely you, if we were awesome at all things. Would you like to be common or unique? I chose unique and I invite comparison to get on out. We each wear more hats than we care to, on most any day. My favorite self-proclaimed title is "Cheerleader of the People." I love to encourage my husband, my children, family, employees, friends, peers, and ALWAYS the underdog. This hat is worn all while being a personal shopper, chef, worshipper, writer, finder of all lost things, child, mother, sister, mediator, aunt, friend, delivery driver, and let's not forget the never-ending role of housekeeper and therapist. This list could continue for pages, as I am sure yours could as well. We are vitally important! I am grateful to have the relationships in my life that create opportunity for these titles. It's what has shaped me into me! Now I can't say I always enjoy wearing all the hats. Sometimes I am not in the mood to be "therapist", but when the phone rings and the moment is upon me, I am glad to be able to encourage and speak life over the people I care about. It often comes unexpectedly and is undoubtedly messy, but I know it's where the melody is calling me. It's my time to move, meet a need, and create a positive impact. This may not be your space to shine, but that's all in the beauty. Your strength is needed right where you are. Walk confidently in that.

What area are you uniquely called to shine on? If you're not sure, the comparison trap is set in fertile soil and laying down deep roots. Your inspiration and vision are being stolen day by day. To put that erosion to a stop, take a moment to ask yourself a few simple questions to help you identify your territory!

1. What do you seem to innately know? This may be something which is obvious to you, but appears to be more challenging for others?
2. What do people call on you to get your insight or help with?
3. What do you enjoy doing, developing, or teaching others?
4. What are you able to help people understand, which has been a block for them previously?

You may have my missing eye for style (If so, please return it!), a knack with children, or creativity in the kitchen. Whatever you are good at, walk confidently in that domain, and claim it as your thing! This doesn't need to be something that leads to world peace or generates great wealth for it to be significant. Anything that builds your confidence and allows you to take some ground in your own mind is significant. You do have a thing. You already rock at it; you may simply be failing to recognize it! Identify it. Be bold about what you possess, with an ability to enhance the lives of your fellow dancers. As you discover one area in which you are excellent, you will build confidence in yourself and find you are more willing to be more adventurous in exploring others. You have a territory that is yours to oversee and welcome others into, but first you must identify what you rock and the rest (and much more) will fall into place. Make this the beginning of your song and get to moving with it!

There is another important aspect of walking in the melody of the mess, and that is being mindful of who is setting the beat. You know that old saying, "She walks to the beat of her own drum."? Be that chick. Do that. **Walk to the beat of your drum**. You know what is true and important for you. As we fight to defeat the assassin that is comparison, it's also important to note that in our insecurities we can allow ourselves to be influenced by opinions and directions given by others. There are times requiring us to seek wise advice, but far too often critiques are given when not requested, by people who do not have the expertise to warrant their input. Worse than that, often criticism is RECEIVED as fact when it should be rejected, as an opinion we don't agree with. This can be distracting noise taking us off our path. Once you have a vision and your inspiration is flowing, don't let the negative input from others impact your plan. There is nothing wrong with adjusting based on changes or new experience but use caution in how much weight you give to thoughts from people with no skin in your game, or to keep with the music and dancing theme, sweat in this choreographed routine! Be bold enough to honestly assess the source and any underlying motives that may accompany negative feedback. Remember this is your thing, your baby, and you get to decide the direction. Do not give your power away.

The importance of authenticity is beyond what I can communicate. The problem with being authentically me is that I must first know myself. I must deal honestly and gracefully with me. You must do the same. We must stop being so harsh and critical that we overlook what is good and right, just as it is. We must also acknowledge where we need adjustments, because we all have areas for growth. This is not an indictment of our character or indication of inadequacy, but rather a place for us to assign attention, to make ourselves stronger. Being able to gently and lovingly assess our "pitchy-ness and flat notes" is a gift we deserve. We can't assess ourselves against the measuring stick of someone else but must gauge against our own standard. Am I ever going to have the abs and booty I had in high school? Quite unlikely. I have had children and I think I mentioned that I quite enjoy chocolate. I have taken steps to improve my health, being more active and making more consistently healthy choices where I avoid sugar most days. I am at a healthy BMI and I feel more wonderful than I have in the last 20 years. This is me looking honestly at my physical body, being realistic, showing myself grace (for stretch marks and cellulite, you have some too, right?), but identifying that action steps are required for me to live my life to fullest capacity. Can you give that a shot for me (it's really for you)? I know **we are all great at finding fault within ourselves, but would you be willing to add a grace lens to that evaluation**?

The grace for ourselves allows us to take down the shroud of shame we too often hide beneath. People are so used to seeing the highlight reel of other people's lives that the glimpse into authenticity is refreshing and draws them into what we offer. Do we need everything polished and filtered before it's picture worthy? I am so over that. We have already established that life is messy. It's not picture perfect. In this we all agree, but it seems like we all believe life should be photo shopped into a fairytale and that is continuing the comparison trap! I don't want to see fake and altered reality. I am drawn to transparency and authenticity in people. Let me be clear though, I am not talking about harsh, blunt, ugliness. I mean the funny stuff we all relate to. Laughing at ourselves for tripping over the curb on the way into the office or rushing out of the house and forgetting deodorant and needing to check myself periodically throughout the day so I don't accidently become the stinky adult before I make it to the store and buy a new stick! Or the hard stuff that we are battling our way through and sharing our journey minus the pity party. Let's admit we don't have it all together, but we are doing our best to get it figured out. There is no shame in that. **If we are doing our best, we will make it through, and the bonus is we can help others believe they will too.**

Knowing what core beliefs make up the character and reputation you choose to be known for will help with decisions in all areas of life. You will have the opportunity to cut corners, leave out facts, and skirt around an issue that needs to be addressed. The fact remains that often, it's impossible to be true to ourselves and do what is popular among the masses. A synonym of popular is common, and our core beliefs are likely not common. This is good because remember, you are unique! We are not aiming to lower our standards or conform to what is popular. We should be skipping along to our own drum and setting the standard by which we operate. I can't tell you what your standard should be, just like you can't tell me mine. This is for you to decide, and it's something that you must not only determine for yourself, but you must use in all areas. Core beliefs don't get to take the day off for business, or for a big-ticket sale you need to make, or for this one tricky parenting situation. They are tied to the core of what is true for you, in all areas of life. I have personally had to make difficult decisions about relationships that were unhealthy for me. It wasn't that I didn't enjoy the person or find certain aspects of our relationship a bright spot in my life, but rather due to characteristics that were in direct opposition to what I stand for and/or boundaries being crossed. Likewise, I have ceased to work with individuals that did not provide a promised service to a client. When my name and my reputation are associated, it is important to me that integrity is strong. This meant hard conversations were in order, ones I would have preferred to quietly ignore (like a third-grade boy ignores his crush!). What we are confident in will surely be challenged, but don't let it compromise the integrity of your vision. Walk in truth, operate in integrity, and know you will have to remain steadfast about these types of decisions, when the time comes. What is popular should not be of concern when it comes to core beliefs; popular for products and services you want to provide, I'll give you, but your **core beliefs must be solid and transcend all areas of life for us to have congruency and authenticity.**

You lady are strong and incredibly smart. You are also sensitive and that is an awesome attribute. **Your sensitivity combined with intelligent strength is a beautiful gift just on the other side of a hurdle!** As women we are naturally more in tune with the feelings of others, and, we like to do all we can to ensure others are whole, and their needs are being met. Aren't we sweet? This can easily go sideways and create a downward spiral to out of control. This is something we must keep at the forefront of our minds, and something we need to actively manage. Compassion is a human emotion I would like to see catch on like steaming music has replaced CDs, BUT there is a thin line between being in tune with other's emotions and having expectations tied to what emotions we are looking for. There is also a control and manipulation aspect that can be exploited against us, or by us. Let's work not to be the girl using control or being controlled! I just said a lot. This is the single hardest piece of choreography I have ever attempted to nail. It may just be me, but I have a feeling that you relate to this too. We may be wearing many hats and managing the details of various segments of other people's worlds, but we have zero control over what mood someone else is in. We cannot take the credit, nor the blame, for the joy or lack thereof, within our people's lives. Again, let's accept responsibility to do our best, and to deliver what we promise. We will benefit from being aware of the emotional responses of others, but we must not own their emotions. They belong to them and we have every right to refuse a transfer of negative energy!

The downward spiral to crazy land is just around the corner, when we tie our expectations to the emotional responses of others. Take a tiny trip with me, won't you? Let's just say a hypothetical woman (ME!) goes out of her way to make a hypothetical employee feel special for her birthday. Maybe this employee is a wife and mom who shares that she doesn't get treated like the queen she would like on special days, since she had her baby. I may have identified what her favorite home cooked meal was and made it from SCRATCH. I also may have gone above and beyond to get others to pitch in for a gift card to her favorite boutique and invited other people to come celebrate a surprise lunch at her office. This was, by all accounts, a lovely display of unexpected, unrequired, and selfless kindness. Hypothetically (because I don't want to admit this happened, in my head), I may have been disappointed with the mild show of appreciation for the special day I created. I may have had to fight off irritation every time I saw her for the next week. How dare her gratitude level not hit the right mark on the appreciation scale! That is so insane. She didn't ask for this birthday treat, and I put it together because I wanted her to know that I thought she was special. Mission accomplished, and message sent. If I didn't want to go through the hassle of doing this, then I should not have done so. We need to be mindful in evaluating our own motives when we are doing nice things or paying compliments to others. Are we doing this because we want to, and we value what they offer, or are we doing it to create a payoff? If our motives are pure, we should not have mood fluctuations and frustrations tied to another person's joyfulness or other expected response. This is tough. I catch myself getting ready to jump on the crazy spiral sometimes and must remind myself that it's not a fun ride. Skip that one! When I do or say something nice, it's because I wanted to be kind, meet a need, or lift someone's spirits, or because I love their shirt, not because I am attempting to illicit similar treatment, kudos, or a response.

We must guard our own emotions from being taken hostage by the mood and perceived attitude of others. We choose if we are happy or disgruntled. Have you ever been bopping along having a great day when you get a phone call from someone you love and find they are not in the same head space? By the time you get off the phone your mood is about half as good as it was before that phone call. You can almost hear "Wah-Wah-Wah" sound playing in your ears. You ma'am have just been mood zapped. It's an awful thing to do to people, or to have done to you. As much as you may not want to hear this, you are likely the zapper as often as you are the zap-ee. That's a hard realization. It's an ugly ride, a mood zapping, downward spiral kind of cycle and it must be broken! Our moods don't have to fluctuate up and down based on the day that other's experience. They shouldn't if you want to be the strong and stable woman you are capable of being.

Again, compassion is a powerful human emotion, and I am all for showing love and support to those we encounter and influence, but we must protect ourselves in the process. Give love, offer help when you can, be a listening ear if your heart can handle that weight, but don't take the weight of the burden of someone else, and make it your own. You can't afford to carry yours and everyone else's too. You know what you can handle and what you can't, and your threshold is your own. You can't be the woman you need to be and get your mission accomplished if you are the pack mule of other's emotional baggage. Your mood and your joy levels are your responsibility. And their mood and their joy levels are theirs. Be cautious about letting your special someone (child, mom, spouse, boss, etc.) be the mood setter. That is dangerous and gives away control that we should be protecting. That special someone needs you whole and healthy. Your heart is serious business and it needs you to take good care of it, on a constant basis. The world is full of all kinds of people with all kinds of circumstances, good and bad. Ensure the random encounters of your day don't set your mood music. Your happiness is far too important to leave it to chance.

You and I have a calling and purpose. We are each unique and special, and our action and ownership of our power is so desperately needed in the world we're walking through. I challenge you to stop looking down and judging yourself harshly against the unrealistic measuring stick you have been using. Instead, hold your head up high and give yourself some credit for the challenges you have already overcome. Evaluate where you could be a little stronger this time next month, even while realizing that you are sitting amid blessings you can touch; be grateful for that position. Assess where you are a leader and can help others be more fabulous with some guidance from you, and then confidently do that. Your ability to be strong and sensitive to the emotional needs of others can be used like a radar detector to place you where you are needed and to thrive. You have a beautiful set of standards that will set you apart and allow you to make a difference right where you are. Let this breathe life into your vision and create inspiration for how you can use the gifts you already possess. Use this intentionally to create a positive impact on both the chosen special few you touch daily, and the random unknowns you will see in the coming days. Take that calling seriously and continue to grow into the woman you were created to be. It's worth the effort and will help you find the melody in the messiness of life. You are where you belong in this season and you have places to go, in the days ahead.

AMIE POUGES

Amie is a southern girl born and raised in a small town north of Dallas; she believes hospitality and sweet tea could go a long way in making the world a better place. She is the oldest of three girls and has played the role of caretaker and nurturer from the time she became a big sister, at four years old. Amie's most treasured titles are those of wife, mother, and friend. Encouraging and mentoring women is a passion she discovered early in her career, when she took on her first management position. Professionally she has been a banker for over twenty years, recently taking on the role of corporate trainer, developing and facilitating curriculum on the best practices of lending. Amie is a busy wife and mother who loves to spend time with her family, cook and create new recipes, and actively attend and volunteer at her church. To feed her passion, she loves hosting friends in her home, writing, and encouraging women through her personal blog "She Longs to Belong."

- https://www.facebook.com/SheLongsToBelong/
- https://www.instagram.com/shelongstobelong/
- https://www.linkedin.com/in/amie-pouges-76857b55/

CATHY HAGEMAN, LE
Learning Who I AM

I have never written a book or been a co-author of a book. In fact, I really don't like writing. I rather get to know someone and then tell my story a little at a time. Yes, I am a pretty private person. I like getting to know other people, what's going on in their lives - the good and the bad. Maybe it is a diversion tactic to my own life.

My life, for the most part, has been uneventful. I was raised in the typical American family. My parents were married 47 years. I always said my parents were a combined force. My sister and I couldn't get away with anything and we could never play the game of "well mom said its ok or dad said its ok" Don't get me wrong, I loved my parents - maybe too much. They were my everything. I pulled them into every relationship and every decision. Their voices were continuously echoing in my head. I was sheltered growing up and didn't have a lot of friends. I was the "good girl" at school. I played by the rules and didn't want to cause problems.

Because I was so close to my parents and sheltered my decisions in life were their decisions. Take college for instance, where I went was primarily based on where they thought best - plus they were paying so really couldn't argue. The college we choose happened to have both a good music program and business program. I thought I wanted to be a music major with a business minor. Unfortunately, since the college, I choose had a well-recognized music program the college didn't encourage the business minor. So, I changed to full business major. I went from a CPA major to a finance major to an education major with a business emphasis. Can you tell I really didn't know what to major in? I just wanted the degree. I wanted to make my parents happy. My dad was well educated so education was important.

In the middle of my sophomore year of college, I moved back

home. I wasn't happy away from my parents. My plan was to finish my basic college courses, get a job and figure out what I wanted to do in life. The next 2 years was a whirlwind of changes. I met my future husband, moved out of my parent's house and eventually married. This was a significant time for me with a lot of changes happening.

Being married, working, going to school is a struggle. Add the stress of wanting to please both your parents and your husband. I still didn't know what I wanted in life.

My husband had done the college thing already. He worked in the family business where a degree wasn't required. The company I worked at during this time didn't encourage me to finish my education. All great excuses for me to use to quit college and figure some stuff out.

So, my journey of who I am began......

Side Note here: Some people know who they are and what they want early on in life. AND the rest of us figure it out later, hopefully not too late in life. Don't be discourage if you are later, there is hope. Keep reading.

I felt I needed help in my journey. I had become such a people pleaser I didn't know who I was or what I wanted. When you get "help" you go through the wonderful process of rehashing up your past - the good, the bad and the ugly.

My parents were Christians when they married and went to church regularly. They stopped attending church after they started our family and we didn't go much until I was 15-16 years old. It was during this time that my dad made some big changes in his life. My dad was a wonderful man, very kind and loving. For me to see changes was huge since I thought he was already great. Those changes impacted my life so much that I became a Christian at 16 years. I wanted to serve God to the fullest! I wanted to do what he called me to do. But that didn't necessarily agree with what my parents wanted.

Part of my challenge or conflict, whatever you want to call it, as I was very close to my parents. I didn't do much without their approval. Any decision I made without approval was met with resistance - Where to go to college, getting married were some big ones.

When I got married that "wanting approval" shifted to my husband. Now in my 20's I am getting inputs from both parents and husband. No wonder I was confused. If I had an idea to do something, I would get everyone's opinion and if anyone didn't agree I wouldn't do.

When I sought help with my discovery, one of the first things I had to do was make a decision without anyone's input. I started with small decisions, so it wouldn't do much harm, like what dog food to buy. I know silly and sad. It was scary but freeing.

Maybe this is you or someone you know. I wasn't a bad person. I could make decisions, , but I lack confidence in myself to voice the decision and be ok with the outcome. I had the fear of failing or being wrong and then getting the "I told you so" speech. No one wants that speech.

All this created underlying anger and resentment. I was angry at myself. Why couldn't I stand up for my thoughts, suggestions or ideas? I had no problem going to bat for someone else. In fact, I try to encourage people and rally behind them when they are pursuing a dream or new venture. I tend to be better doing that for others instead of doing for myself.

As my confidence grew, I left the job I had worked for 12 years to do something else. What?! I didn't know. So, I did contract jobs for one year. I only had a few jobs, but I realized during that time what I didn't want. I finally landed a job at a great company and stayed there several years. During my employment, the company got bought out and as the story goes sometimes, we had to learn to fit into a new and different environment, To say it was stressful was an understatement. We were constantly having to prove ourselves. Perseverance was my middle name. The last project I was on prior to leaving had been a labor of love and perseverance for 4-5 years. I was constantly selling someone on the idea of why we were doing this project, why we needed it, how efficient we would be and the cost savings. All on deaf ears.

Frankly, I got burned out. I wanted to do my own thing, be in control, set my own path. Now, what would I do.......?????

Some people start their own business because they were laid off. They look back at the "blessing in disguise" because they would have never quit to start the business.

Given my background, you would think I would have been one of those people. In fact, I had several people tell me to wait until I was laid off, at least I would get a severance package, etc. I resigned instead. Honestly, I didn't think I was strong enough to be called into a room and let go. That seemed like I had failed when that wasn't the case. Besides, I had seen others let go with no severance package and I wasn't willing to risk that.

But getting back to now what? I didn't quit without knowing the next steps. I am a planner - not a type A planner, but I like to know what's coming next.

I had brainstormed, with my husband, all my likes, and interest. Yes, still working through that decision making from others - it's a process. Some things are no issue for me and other things I still struggle with. Anyways, 2 major interest or loves identified were animals and beauty stuff.

We researched doing the doggie daycare thing. I looked at a couple of businesses to purchase, etc. The locations were ok, but for me the risk was high. I am a huge animal lover and would be devastated if something happened to one of the animals. So, I decided to pass on that idea.

The second idea was beauty stuff. My sister in law is a hair stylist and I have always loved hair, skincare, and makeup. So, we looked at hair salons to purchase. That was rather eye-opening for me. Looking at places, how they looked, cleanliness, the hair stylist, their income statement, etc. all new territory for me. I could look at the income statements with no big issues but the other stuff, rules on sanitation, managing people, licensing was all new to me.

Since I only knew the business side and not the industry itself I figured I better go to school to learn. After much discussion, I went to got an Esthetician license. Why not hair you may ask, well some was the cost of service - how many haircuts would I need to do to make money, plus did I want to stand on my feet all day and last it would take a good year to get my license. The state of Texas requires 1500 hours for Cosmetology license (1 full year) and 750 hours for Esthetician license (5-6 months). Also, at the time the med spa's had become popular and I thought I had the potential to make better money going that route.

Looking back and knowing what I know now, I might advise someone to go for the Cosmetology license since it gives you more options for services. Cosmetology license gives hair, skin, and makeup. Granted many of the education hours are in hair, ~ 200-300 in skin and makeup, a person would have more service options once they got the license. Esthetician license is 750 hours of all skin and makeup. If I was advising a person wanting to be an esthetician, I would also advise them to go to dermatology school or be a nurse. The regulations on skin services are increasing as doctors see the profits from cosmetic services versus regular services.

The main reason I went to school was to learn about the industry and the regulations. Otherwise, I would have invested in a business and managed it. I felt I would be at a disadvantage since I knew nothing from an internal process and quality standpoint. I don't regret going. I learned a lot of new things and met some wonderful people, some who I am still friends with today. I would tell anyone that education is a great route to take. Educating yourself on a subject only has its gains no real losses. You get more information on the subject and grow personally.

After my required hours were completed I had to study for the certification. I had decided since I left the corporate world and wanted to be my own boss I would strike out on my own straight out of school.

Two weeks after I got my certification, I signed a lease on a room and flew to Los Angeles, CA for more training at UCLA. Remember I said more training is good. This was a semester class condensed into 3 days of power packed information. My head was swimming. All good stuff but A LOT.

Once back I began the process of setting up my room. When people say they want to go into business, they have seen or admired someone else who either has done it or currently running their own business. This person we admire is seen as successful, has money, answers to no one and has freedom. This is what a lot of people want. This person we watch makes it look so easy and effortless.

#Truth #Reality Starting a business is tough. It is not for the faint of heart. I am not trying to be negative. I am trying to speak the truth. It's a lot of hard work and there are unknowns. I don't mind the hard work, but do mind the unknowns. I didn't mention earlier but my corporate job had been in quality and project management. In that role, I worked with teams to define their day to day processes and tools and create reports to analyze the outputs of those processes. These teams used the data to estimate department budgets and cost savings.   I worked with the management to document process and tool changes on their projects and analyze reports to ensure project costs were on track. Being accountable for someone else's budget is totally different than your own budget. If the budget goes over in the corporate world, that money doesn't come out of your personal account like in your own business.

When I started my business I was naive, in my opinion, on how it would go. I thought I would get a room somewhere, buy my equipment and products, do some decorating and all my friends, family and old co-workers would come to me. I had also gotten a room in a salon suite with other hair stylists - one being my own personal hair stylist - I thought I could get referrals from some of them.

I was using my saving to invest in the business and make my living expenses. I didn't want to get a loan. I had planned for it to be slow to start but using the marketing skills I learned in school that I would get repeat business and new clients to meet my bills. Let's just say what I put on paper and reality didn't match.

Lesson #1 - do your research before starting your own business. I think the more you know the better prepared you will be

Lesson #2 - If you are going into a service business, look to see if they are regulated by the state. If the service is regulated by the state, read the laws and regulations on that service. Check the Texas Department of Licensing and Regulation.

Lesson #3 - Decide where you want your business. Can you do from your house (look at regulations, if applies)? Can you rent an executive suite? Do you need or want retail space? Once you decide this, start visiting these places. Ask how much the rent or lease is. Get a copy of the rent or lease contract - READ IT. How long is your commitment to the lease/rent? What if you need to leave before the end of the contract can you easily or will you need to continue paying? If a retail space - what is the cost of the rent, the maintenance fees, the insurance fees? Retail space has what is called a triple net lease. For example, the rent can be $500 a month, then you add the maintenance cost, the insurance cost, and the real estate taxes, so your $500 a month just jumped to $1000 because of these other costs.

Go visit these places several times during the week. See what the traffic is like around the area. Visit with people that lease there or hang around there. You want a good vibe on where you choose.

Lesson #4 - Start a spreadsheet listing out your cost, including your new workplace. If you can work from home, then that is a blank row on the sheet. List out your supplies needed. Remember supplies will need to be replenished so try to project those cost. If you have a service business at a retail space, you will need business liability insurance and sale taxes possibly. You may need a business lawyer so add that to your list. How will people find you? Add advertising cost to your list. My point is to list it all on a spreadsheet. If you aren't sure the cost, try to find out. Your biggest cost will be the monthly rent/lease and your advertising.

Lesson #5 - Who is your customer? Who is your best client ever? It is interesting, even in my industry not everyone is my customer. I thought that was funny at first because everyone has skin and a lot of people I knew cared about how they look. But even some of those are not my client. They could be, but they aren't. Doing a facial is personable. It's like getting your hair done. Some people will go to a barber or great clips or whoever. Others are very particular on who touches their hair. Some have had bad experiences so are very cautious about who touches their hair. Same thing on skin services. I have had a lot of clients who have had a bad experience. I have had others that liked the facial but came to me because they didn't like the other place they were going. I have some that won't see me because I don't do the medical grade treatments which require a medical director over me, i.e. Injections, Micro-needling, lasers.

Only you can determine who your best client is. This is the client you want for a lifetime. The client that likes you as a person, sees you as the expert and values your profession. You strive to get as many of these types of people as you can. Knowing who is your best client ever will benefit your marketing strategies, so you reach the customer who wants your business. Sometimes the ones who we think will not be our best client are just the ones that are. So, it is important to treat everyone the same - with your highest professionalism.

Lesson #6 - Advertise yourself. The reason you want to know your best client ever is you need people to know you are in business. Advertising is expensive. It will be one of your highest percentage of cost on your spreadsheet. You want to make sure you are spending those dollars wisely, so you get a return on your investment. Sure, you can throw a banner over your retail space so people driving by see it. You can do that, but you may also want to do other advertising as well.

Once you have a good idea of your best client. How do you reach those people? What is the age range of your client? What is their interest? Where do they hang out - gym's, mall, Starbucks, etc. There are so many ways to advertise and when you do go into business you will get all those nice people calling you telling you why their way is best. I can't emphasize enough to DO YOUR RESEARCH.

There are several options for advertising and making people aware of your business:
- Paper advertising. This includes the flyers we get in the mail

to the printed magazine. Paper advertising may or may not work. It depends on your business and the target market age group.

- Social media. Again, which platform does your best client ever use? There are several platforms with new ones coming on the horizon. When you choose this route, consistency is a must. Being camera shy won't do you good, so get over that quickly. Videos rule on several platforms. I am not good at the videos. I hate seeing myself on camera. To succeed in my industry, I need to overcome this quickly.

1. Web pages and Search Engine Optimization (SEO). Creating a webpage for your business is a must. Otherwise, how does anyone find you on their web searches and know what you offer? But creating a webpage is one thing, you must have keywords scattered throughout the site so when people search you show up. This is called SEO. There are companies that can help you with this, but they are not cheap and usually won't guarantee results. You will need to decide if you want to pay for this type of help.

- Radio and TV. Depending on your business this may be an option. Check on the pricing because peak hours are most expensive. Also, consider Pandora or Sirius - if that reaches your potential client.

- Networking Groups or Chamber of Commerce. A great way to practice your 30-60 speech (your elevator pitch on your business). Some people are comfortable doing this and others not so much. It is a good way to test out what works and doesn't work. You also make great contacts that will hopefully refer your business. Check pricing on these as well. Not all networking groups are free. Some network groups only allow one business per category, for example, if you are a roofer they only let one roofing company in the group.

- Soliciting. Pass your business card out to other businesses around you or to people at Starbucks or the mall. Pass out fliers or brochure to other business promoting your business.

- Partner with another business. Find other businesses you can partner with on an event or share a table at a conference. This gives good synergies between businesses. You refer your customers to them and they refer their customers to you. Plus it's more fun planning an event with other businesses. It brings in new ideas and opportunities.

- Events or Conferences. You can plan an event to promote your business. Potential customers get you meet you and it gives you the opportunity to let them know what you offer. Become a subject matter expert in your field. If you are in an executive suite situation you can rent a conference room and host an educational type meeting on a subject within your business. Or if you are chamber member you can use one of their rooms to host one of these events.

Lesson #7 - Name your business. Do you want a business name or use your own name for the business? Depending on what your business is, it may or may not matter. I wanted a business name. I didn't want to use my name. I like to keep my personal stuff separate from my business stuff. I think I came up with a great name for my business. It reflects how I view skincare and it's straight and to the point. If you want to use your name, that is great, go for it. Just know this is an option.

Lesson #8 - Brand/ Logo. You have your name. How do you want the business logo to look? What color(s) will it be? Graphics or pictures? Once all has been decided, get your business cards and brochures or fliers printed. Will you need stationary for your business? Consider getting your logo printed on some.

Lesson #9 - How will the customer contact you? Do you need another phone line? Will you use your current mobile or landline? Before you jump to using your personal cell or landline, think about this.... do you want that "one customer" to have your cell number? Plus, if you are going into a retail space you may want a separate line, so it looks professional. There are lots of options now on this. There are Google numbers and other apps that provide additional numbers without getting another phone to carry.

Lesson #10 - Utilities. Will you need to pay for water, electric, gas or AC if you are renting or leasing? This usually applies to retail spaces, but you may want to consider those cost depending on the service you are offering and where you are offering the service.

Lesson #11 - Supplies, products, and equipment to run your business. What is it going to take to run your business? No matter where you land your business, you will need fundamental supplies to make it all happen. You will most likely need a computer unless you want to put it all on paper and pencil. Will you need a new computer or upgrade the one you currently have? Will you need office supplies like a printer or scanner? If you are a service business, what equipment and supplies will you need? Same with a restaurant or bakery, what equipment and supplies will you need? I created a list of equipment and all my supplies in a spreadsheet. I put the item in one column and the price in the column next to it.

That way I could do a total of everything to get a cost projection.

Lesson #12 - Certifications, Licensing, Permits. Will your business require any city licensing or permits? Will you and your business need any certifications? Depending on the business you may need to post that your business is compliance, so the public can see this. You will also need these if your business gets inspected by the city or state.

After you have researched each consideration, list it on your spreadsheet - the item and the cost. On your spreadsheet add the monthly cost for each item. Some will be an upfront cost, some will be monthly, some quarterly, etc. I highly recommend this even if you are not a budget tracker kind of person. Even with my financial background, I was never good about following a budget. My husband and I figured out other ways to make sure we were saving and not overspending.

I suggest you do all of this prior to quitting your job or starting your business. Why do you ask? I am not trying to discourage you. I want you to have a clear picture going into this business. You see I didn't do this. You will have up days where you are on top of the world, then you also have down days when you feel like a failure. On the down days, you need to remember why you did this, that you expected stuff to happen, that you are not a failure, that it will get better, that you knew this might happen, you had your spreadsheet. See my graphic below showing how I felt.

Friends and family are both good and bad when starting a business. People are quick to tell you that a percentage of businesses fail in the 1st five years of business. You will need to be and feel confident on your numbers yourself and so when someone says something negative you can brush that comment off. I knew some of my cost going in. I had a clear view of my equipment and supplies cost. Thankfully one of my last projects in school was to set up a salon and all the cost around that. So, I had an idea about the equipment needed, supplies needed, and I had researched my lease information.

What I didn't know, and my surprises were, that the clients I thought would come to see me didn't. People that came to support me while I was in school disappeared when I started my business. Why? Honestly, I don't know. But I was on a scramble to get customers to know I existed. Doing a webpage and setting up social media sites are all good things but unless you have followers on social media and good SEO on your site you won't show up on the first page of a web search. I thought I had a well-worded webpage, but organic searches take time. I did Google ad words, direct mail, magazine ads, social media ads, networking and chamber meetings. I got a few new customers out of this combination but no huge return on my investment.

Don't get discouraged yet. Just because some of these did not work well for me doesn't mean it won't well for you. There are several in my industry that have done all or some of these and had great results. There are a lot of dynamics that go into this, so no one can give you the magic bullet. You try something and if it doesn't work you try something else. The beauty of being your own boss is you can change things quickly without anyone's approval. Something else I did when I was in school was join industry and marketing groups on Facebook. This was quite helpful. There are many people that offer great advice and encouragement. Depending on your industry you may also find mentors within the industry that offer great advice on starting a business and their experiences.

I will caution that even though social media provided a lot of great information, I had to be careful not to compare myself to other people. Because I value others inputs, a little too much, I compared myself to others in the industry and wondered why things I did same as they didn't result in the same way.

Like I said earlier on the advertising, some got a lot of clients from their local chamber or networking group. I didn't have the same experience. That doesn't mean it doesn't work and don't do it, it means for me it wasn't the silver bullet. Also, several in my industries have a lot of friends and family as clients. Again, for me, that did not happen. My point is you get advice from others then decide the best approach for you. It may work great for you! It also may need to be tweaked for you. Don't put yourself in a box. A lot of times in business we must get out of our comfort zone. I personally don't like speaking in front of large groups. I prefer the small groups. I have had to push myself out of this and I am still working on this.

Owning your own business has its rewards. Freedom for one. But it can be challenging, frustrating and there are late nights at times. It's like a roller coaster ride, lots of highs and lows. The better you are prepared for this the better you will make it through the lower times. Remember, even if it doesn't work the first time out the gate, keep trying, keep moving forward, keep looking and trying new things. Remember several now wealthy business people failed several times before they finally made it. You can do this!

CATHY HAGEMAN, LE

Cathy Hageman is a Texas licensed esthetician and spa owner. She takes a holistic approach to her skin services. Per Cathy, "Anything that shows up on your skin is usually caused by internal and/or external factors". Cathy stays current on beauty industry trends and cutting-edge products by continued education through UCLA and beauty industry classes. Cathy is passionate about finding the most natural, non-invasive, healthy products available to bring out the natural, luminous skin for each client. She especially enjoys seeing client skin transformation and how happy her clients are with their results. Cathy has contributed to an article in Lifestyle Frisco and is a member of the Frisco Chamber of Commerce.

For more information on her spa, go to www.skinbasix.com.

- Facebook - https://www.facebook.com/cathyhagemanbiz/
- Instagram - https://www.instagram.com/skinbasix/
- Twitter - https://twitter.com/SkinBasix
- LinkedIn - https://www.linkedin.com/in/cathy-hageman-622a91/
- Pinterest - https://www.pinterest.com/skinbasix/

SUSAN JONES
Journey of a Wave Maker

I was born and brought up in India until I got married and moved to the greatest country in this world, the United States of America. I have heard my parents share, that my birth was a miracle. My mom would vomit blood while she was pregnant with me. I was born post-mature, meaning I was born way after my due date. According to my mom, she was not feeling any movement of the baby and her parents took her to the hospital. On reaching the hospital, the X-ray showed that I was turning blue and had only a few hours left before I was going to be stillborn. So, the doctor rushed my mom to the operating table because they were running against time. The first anesthesia administered gave my mom an allergic reaction, so they had to stop it and find the right one. It was a life and death situation for the mom and the baby.

During this time, my dad was way in the central part of India working in the steel plant. My grandparents were communicating with my dad via telegram, which in those days took several days to send and receive a reply. Looking back, I sometimes wonder how we lived without cell phones. So, my grandparents and uncles decided to make a decision on behalf of my dad. I remember my grandmother telling me when I went to visit her after my marriage, that my grandfather came home and prayed that God would keep me alive because a child was born in his house after a 20-year gap and that he would dedicate me for the work of the lord if I survived and made it through this ordeal.

I was given four hours to live after my birth, I was told, that the only reason the doctors even tried to treat me was that they heard me making a sighing noise, so they decided to give me some blood. My maternal uncle volunteered to donate his blood. My early childhood included frequent visits to the hospital. In those days, there were no daycare facilities, so I was left with my grandparents to be raised by them. My parents would come to visit me during the summer vacation time. My mom was a teacher, so during her summer break they would come and stay for a few weeks with me. When I was ready to start school, my parents came and took me to stay with them. I was four years old when it happened, and I hated the fact that I couldn't be with my grandparents all the time. Looking back, I think I was spoiled by my grandparents, aunts, and uncles.

As a three-year-old, I remember watching my grandpa wake up early in the morning and praying with my grandma. After his prayer, my grandpa would take a walk around his property asking God to bless the works of his hands. Once he returned from his walk, he would wake everyone up for the morning family prayer. Prayer was a central part of my grandparent's lives until they went home to be with Jesus. I am so thankful that what the enemy meant for harm, God used for HIS good. I watched my grandpa do all kinds of business endeavors and succeed in it. I am sure, there were days of frustrations because things may not have quite gone the way it should have, but I remember him thanking God, during our evening family prayer, for the good day grandpa had.

My grandpa had a coffee, rubber plantation among other crops that he planted. He was very successful at whatever he did, and I learned, watching him that I can to do any business and be successful at it. It would take work in the initial stages but eventually, it would start working for me.

It all changed, when I came to stay with my parents as a four-year-old. The life with my parents was very different. I felt rejected by my father because I was not a boy. My father would physically abuse me and growing up under domestic violence started making me physically sick again. Some days I couldn't go to school. I had more memory of being in the hospital than being in school in my early days of education. I recall a time when I was in the hospital for a period of 3month. One of those months, I had a severe case of chicken pox and I was transferred to the isolation unit with IV running through my arms. While in the isolation unit, one day my fever spiked, and I had a seizure and my body convulsed, and I thought I died. Years later, during one of my complaining sessions with the Lord, HE showed me a vision of that day. In the vision, I saw one of the pastors that conducted our wedding kneeling beside my bed and praying for my healing and dedicating me to the Lord's work. It almost seemed, like I had died but was brought back to life. When you have experienced a near-death situation your perspective on life changes.

At the age of ten, I was attending a church convention at our home church, a Pastor stood up and spoke about heaven and hell. That night, I made the decision to accept Christ as my personal savior and the healing process in my body began. Even though my healing began, the beating didn't stop. The last time I was in the hospital was before I got water baptized at the age of 15. Since then, it's been a journey with HIM.

I hated life at a young age, but when I would read the BIBLE for instance in Deuteronomy 31:6 "Be strong and of good courage, do not fear nor be afraid of them; for the Lord your God, He is the One who goes with you. He will not leave you nor forsake you." (NKJV). I remember thinking If the word says HE will never leave me, where was God now when I needed him most. I felt like, GOD was lying to me.

I grew up thinking, no one will even want me and that I was a loser and I am fat and would never mount up to anything in life.

Unfortunately, this is what my dad would constantly say to me. I now know that Satan was using my dad to speak lies but I thank GOD that during it GOD was faithful. Just know, Satan would make you believe that you are all those things because he will make it look and sound like, it's you are speaking those words to yourself in your own voice.

In school, my classmates called me an elephant because I was heavy for my size. I was unable to do a lot of activity without having to stop midway or collapse in the middle of it. Did I mention, I used to take medications like I was eating food, three times a day. As you know, all medications have side effects, one of them is gaining weight. Being bullied was normal for me. The only difference being, where I grew up it was ok to be bullied because the culture says women are just doormats. Fortunately, things have changed a lot as the younger generations are getting more educated.

I grew up in the church but in a very religious setting, there were tons of don'ts than dos. The relationship aspect was never taught. So, I would just go to church because that's what we did on Sunday's. But I never had a real relationship with the LORD till I was a teenager. The constant beatings, emotional, mental and verbal abuse continued while attending the church. For years we prayed for our dad, and God did change my dad in his old age because of a life-altering surgery he had. My dad never thought he would survive that surgery.

Due to this constant physical abuse, I had a hard time relating to God as a good father. Because I felt, HE was never there for me during my dark days. Unfortunately, for a lot of us, we don't know how to relate to our heavenly father because of the way our earthly father treats us. I grew up with a skewed ideology about God. I had no problem having a relationship with Jesus and the Holy Spirit. As a young child, I was told by my family to never speak out of the things I have gone through in the house since it would be shameful and bring dishonor to the family. In addition, the enemy would say no one will believe you, you will bring disgrace to the family. I grew up thinking and wondering if there would ever be an end to this torment. This led me to attempt suicide multiple times. I was tired of the manipulation tactics that my dad, mom, and my sister would use as I got older to keep me quiet. As I look back, it is the grace of God that helped and kept me from killing myself. I grew up thinking no one will even hear me, I would be just a number. My dad is right, I will just exist, will never be at a place of influence. Why would God want me on this earth? There were many nights I would cry myself to sleep asking God to take my life. I would ask GOD, What's the purpose of so much pain in my life? And why me? At the same time, I am asking WHY? I kept reading my BIBLE and I would say to GOD if you can use me for HIS kingdom then use me. Even though I would ask GOD to use me in my teen year, I was full of anger and doubt during my teenage years. On one hand, I wanted to do nothing with this being called God, but then for some reason, I also knew it's HIM who is keeping me alive. My faith got stronger after I went to college, away from my parents and I had my time with God. In my college days, instead of studying for my school a lot of the times I would just read my BIBLE and go to sleep. Then in my sleep, I would see a dream. In the dream, GOD would give me twelve questions to study and out of them, six would be in the final exams. That's when I started believing, that God really loves me, and HE was there all along.

After college, I got married to the best person in this entire world, my husband John. He is a man of prayer and faith. Our marriage was arranged according to Indian tradition, To convert to today's dating world, we knew each other for less than an hour before we got married. My father in law, lovingly called daddy, was the best dad anyone could have asked for. Through different dreams I had seen, I knew he was not going to be with us for long, but then there is always the wishful thinking process of longing to have him around. Today I am thankful for the time I had to spend with him before I came to the states to be with my husband.

After I came to states, I decided to go through the Gary Whetstone School of Biblical Studies which was part of the church we attended in DE. I would recommend the school to anyone out there especially the class called your liberty in Christ. I would write letters to daddy sharing the things I had learned in the BIBLE school. Once daddy passed away, my mother in law shared that, daddy would use my letters as his sermon notes to teach and preach to his congregation. Six months prior to daddy passing away, one day while calling my in-laws, my sister in law had sarcastically teased me by saying it seems like someone suddenly has more faith than everyone. Right then, daddy took the phone from her and he spoke over me that I would write many books and would go around the world and speak to large crowds.

Those words were spoken by my daddy I cherish and recall when I feel all alone and don't think I would be able to take another step. Those words have helped me to forge through my life. When daddy passed away, I couldn't grieve much because I was pregnant with our first daughter. It was a blur. I am thankful for the church family that stepped in to help us during that time. Our pastors stepped into the role of a parent for us. I don't think, we would have survived if Dr. Gary did n't have made us focus back on our purpose for which we got married. He kept speaking over our life what God was showing him about us.

Today, God has blessed us with three kids on this side of the heaven and three in heaven. The two I remember are the ones that happened in 2010. I was very confused as to why this misfortune happened to me. After having two healthy children with no complications, why did I lose two children back to back at 14 weeks? But I just rest in the fact that God knew what we could handle. My awesome gynecologist performed genetic testing on the tissues and he mentioned, the first one I miscarried Feb 26th, 2010 tested positive for downs syndrome and the second one I miscarried on September 25th, 2010, tested for Trisome18. If you ask, Did I go into a deep depression and did I aks lots of WHY? Yes! In 2013 God gave us a healthy boy. We have three healthy kids, 2 girls, and a boy.

You may think, what does this story has anything to do with the business that I do? At a young age growing up with my grandparents, I always wanted to be my own boss. Because I saw a successful businessman in my grandpa. Even though it looked like I had lost it all, God was amid it all. Due to being sick all the time and taking all different types of medication and having tons of side effects. I was determined to find out, how they made those pills, so I studied pharmacology. Then I pursued an MBA, so I can figure out how to be a business owner. After coming to states I worked in a pharmacy till my second daughter was born. Once she was born I stayed home and investigated how to start a nutrition class because of the knowledge that I have. I preferred more natural, holistic way than the traditional medicine. We found out that my husband, had high cholesterol so, instead of putting him on any drugs we reduced his cholesterol with just diet and exercise. We also introduced awesome supplements, that was more potent, and it was formulated in such a way that it got into your system faster, ISOTONIC.

Growing up I remember saying to God, I want to work for three years and then, once I get married, I would like to stay home and be there when kids came home from school, be there at all the school functions and sports activities etc. I wanted to have a relationship with my kids, I am so thankful I get to be part of our kid's life daily. We homeschool our kids. I truly believe in relationship parenting that dictatorial form of parenting.

I knew I would be extremely successful as a business owner, because of the role model that I saw in my grandpa. His biggest success came from trusting God with all his heart, mind and soul. God directed him in every step of the way. I started trusting God the way my grandpa did but had a lot of growing up to do on my part. You may ask, what you mean by that. I stopped believing that I am worth anything, all the things my parents spoke over me was speaking louder than what God had spoken over me. As you may or may not know, words are powerful; Proverbs 18:21 declares death and life are in the power of the tongue, and those who love it will eat its fruit. I had to deal with a lot of negativity in my life.

Due to health problem, we were looking to change our lifestyle, and wanting to take more natural and science-based products I started researching and got introduced to the Direct Sales model. The company I selected was modelled as one to one marketing method; when you spoke with an individual, you give them suggestions on what they can do to achieve their health goals. This included both   be weight loss and/or wanting to have an optimum, overall health. It was very much like a franchise with a working system in place, but without all the overhead of a franchise owner. There is nothing wrong with being a franchise owner, but I knew that with the resources we had to work, this would fit my family schedule and allow me to continue to stay home with my kids. While

I was building my un-franchised business, I was also working as an admin for the Bible school of the church we were part of in Delaware. I loved my admin work because I got to impact many lives for HIS kingdom and encourage and guide students into their God-given purpose. Unfortunately, the miscarriages of 2010 started taking a huge emotional toll and I started to second guess myself. Slowly doubt and discouragement set in. I thought the leadership would step in as they have always preached. My immediate upline was there for me, she did as much as she could to help me, but the directors above her were nowhere to be seen, I was devastated. The team I had worked to build, decided to quit one by one because they saw that I could no longer help. It really did wound my soul that I gave up my dream of being a business owner. Looking back, one thing I learned from this experience is, look for someone, who is secure in their calling and position to follow.

While struggling through these things, my husband, who has an employee mindset, started reminding me that my business will not sustain us for long. I guess, he was looking at the business as an employee rather than as an entrepreneur would see. I don't blame him for that, since he had seen failed business in both the sides of his parent's families. I just knew, that if I can be consistent then we can succeed.

In 2011, we moved to Texas. It was the best decision t we made in our life. My husband is an alumni of UNT so, he always wanted to, move to Texas. As soon as God opened that door we made the move. After we moved, I looked at the business again, because I was determined to prove that a business can pay our mortgage and bills. My husband was okay with the idea since he wanted to see me happy. I went for a breakfast networking meeting at McKinney Tx business chamber and heard this awesome person giving a commercial about a jewelry company. It peaked my interest even though I didn't wear much jewelry due to my traditional Pentecostal background. My first piece of jewelry was my wedding ring that my husband gave me once I came to the US.

As a hobby, I made my own jewelry but mainly to give them away. I made them for the people, that volunteered with me at the church. Each one of them would say I should sell it. I would make them whenever I got time, but then as I kept thinking about it, decided to convert my little hobby into a business. I wanted to do this, so I can have an avenue to empower other women. The model I was thinking was more like a Direct Sales model, so we won't have a lot of overhead costs and any profit margin will go into a foundation with funds to; support orphans and orphanages, help with the rehab of the wounded soldiers, taking care of the children, widows of martyrs for the cause of Christ.

I started praying for the vision and in 2012, Elizabeth, my premier designs upline, invited me to attend a meeting where they were sharing a lot more about this company that she is part of. When I heard their philosophy and purpose, it made perfect sense to me to not reinvent the wheel but join with the company. I came home all excited and shared with my husband. One of my husband's hesitation was with the leadership, His ask was, What's the guarantee that if life happens again, the leaders will be there to support you. But I knew in my gut that I should join the company. So, in September 2013, nine months after the birth of our son I joined Premier Designs high fashion jewelry company.

I haven't looked back ever since. I love the leadership I am under. God has used Premier to rebuild my confidence and has pushed me to seek God's face on a much different level. At our national convention Mr. Andy, Co-Founder of Premier Designs jewelry would always say God did not make an anybody, God made you a somebody. My husband has seen a difference in me in the last five years I have been with the company. John now sees the importance of having our own business. Since being in Premier, we have taken an international trip, fully paid in cash. Last two Christmases has been debt free. My leader who is an awesome friend and family has been there every step of the way. I am so thankful to be part of the company that teaches us servant leadership. I am not all the way there, but life is a journey. I am enjoying the journey I am in at this moment. Have been able to be part of every activity that my children are part of. I get to taxi them for their activities, some days are tiring but, in the end, it's worth every tear and sweat.

I love the direct sales model for a couple of reasons:

•**Relationship-** the relationships you build in direct sales is priceless. I have people that have become friends, I would have never met if I was not in direct sales. It's a family that you gain when you join a direct sale, everyone wants you to succeed and encourage you to do so. You can promote to the next level as many times as you want and as fast as you want because there is enough room for everyone to achieve success. Representatives can grow at their own pace and create their own definition of success. You meet other likeminded people that have already gone before you.

•**Flexibility and income opportunity-** the time flexibility I have with my home base business. I don't have to wait till 5 pm to run to the grocery store or even late at night. I like shopping when it's not too crowded, so I choose to go after 9 pm if the store is open 24hrs. I get to take my kids to swim and piano practices, competitions. In 2017 I took my second daughter for her national competition in swimming. Very proud of her achievement. I didn't have to wait to see if I will be approved to take time off. The company that I am with, I don't need to have an inventory, also there are no quotas to meet. What our company tells us is the fact that I cannot tell my personal recruit to get out and do three shows when I have not even one. So basically, follow by example. The best part was while I was in Michigan I was still able to make money on the world wide web.

•**Recognition** -everyone loves to be recognized but sometimes in a corporate world your efforts may go unnoticed. Not in the direct sales world. I am recognized for every small progress and big progress that you make in business and life. You get to earn free vacations.

•**Business skills** - Direct sales business will help me learn many different business skills that will help you in all areas of your life. There is no better training for someone looking to develop multiple skill sets. Being a homeschool mom I thought I knew, how to juggle the home-based business and homeschooling but I got a rude awakening after the first three months of being in the business. I learned how to manage my time and stay organized. I also learned presentation, and speaking skill, money management, how to do the shows, effectively coach my first level. How to provide the best customer service possible. These skills not only came in handy with the business but also helped me in the day to day things I did. Of course, I am not standing in front of the people every day, but it gave me the confidence I needed to be of help with the Chamber of commerce in our city.

•**Personal Growth**- along with gaining the business skill needed to function in life. It brings transformation in your personal life. I am not the one to stand in front of people and talk. I am more of a one to one versus one to many. Being in the direct sales business, it gave me a boost in my confidence level that I lacked before. I believed in myself and saw a change in how I saw myself. I now look for an opportunity to encourage and pray for someone else. I have seen the grace of God steps in and carries me when I was a week in the areas that I needed to grow.

•**Mentor-** I have been able to mentor others to reach their full potential and see their dreams come to pass. Also, to have someone as a mentor to keep accountable and reach my goals. Indirect sales, you are in the business for yourself but by yourself. The mentor that you have in the business is there when you go through rough spots and when cheer you on when you have reached your goal. That was one thing I looked for when I decided to give the DS a second chance, I knew what kind of leader I want to be under. The awesome part is you get to choose your upline instead of the corporate world, whether you like your manager or not you have no choice but to work under that person.

•**Products** – Direct sales companies carry have the best products out there. You get to buy the products at a wholesale rate instead of full retail and when you solve someone's problem you get paid. Isn't that awesome. You are the first one to see the newest product that's being released. You get to taste the product first if it's a health and wellness product. For me it's jewelry so I get to touch and play in it before it's on the world wide web. I get to see the newest trends that are coming out.

•**Tax benefits, relationships that last a lifetime, personal development and more.** For my personal development was huge. I rediscovered myself, my passion to empower others and developing the gift that God placed within to function in its full potential and not allowing someone to suppress it nor taken advantage of.

In conclusion, I would like to share this quote, "If your WHY is strong enough- you will figure out the HOW"- Bill Walsh. Always remember you are one step closer to your next breakthrough. Each struggle is a stepping stone to success. No dream is so big, that the one who created you, can't bring it to pass. You can do all things through HIM who gives you the strength.

I am looking forward to empowering each woman I come across and take as many that want to come with me to the top. I am building a team of women that would build a family unit, that a person can trust, is integral and would love to serve other and dare to be a difference maker.

SUSAN JONES

I am a wife and a mom to three exceptional children – two daughters and one son. I worked as a pharmacist and have an MBA in marketing. We moved to Texas 7yrs ago and have not looked back. Always dreamed of being a stay home mom. Premier has also allowed me to able to not only meet the financial needs of my family, achieve personal goals and be involved in my community through the Greater Anna Chamber of Commerce. I received a letter from Congressman Sam Johnson's office congratulating me on receiving the Ambassador of the year 2017 award. I and my husband were taped to be part of the marriage curriculum called, "Love and Respect- The Crazy Cycle". So thankful for the flexibility and the freedom Premier has provided. Love to coach and mentor others to do the same and be Successful as well. God's plan is always perfect.

- https://www.facebook.com/NYCFineGems?hc_location=ufi
- https://www.linkedin.com/in/nycfinegems/

NICOLE LYNN

Decluttering of Your Mind

It has been an honor to lead this phenomenal group of ladies I call Wave Makers. When I was presented to compile a book, I was so EXCITED and could not wait. I pictured every lady in the group and the story I felt she needed to share popped into my head. When it came to me, I was like AGH what do I talk about?

Like most ideas with me, it occurred to me after a Monday meeting while I was driving. The never-ending question of confusion – You're an organizer – why are you having a "master-mind" {the closest thing people can relate Wave Makers to}. I always answer with, one of the crucial steps that are missed in organizing is decluttering of the mind, the collection of other people's organizing habits, the rigidness of ideas, the thoughts and fears of perfectionism, shame, and my life is a s*i* show. One of the big challenges of owning your own business is the ownership of all the decisions. When you work for someone else, the negative thoughts and fears aren't as apparent. You're working for someone, and unless you are the owner, there is usually someone above you that is giving you direction. You are not 100% responsible for decisions. When you are the owner – oh how that changes – every decision is YOU, and every consequence to that decision is YOU. This is when the little bags of self-doubt, lack of confidence, worry, fear, and OH-MY's show up in a BIG way. Mental items of clutter can be paralyzing. This led me to talk about the Decluttering of Your Mind!

Paralyzing Fear & Worry:

Fear implies anxiety, loss of courage, and fear of the unknown. I feel this is a reasonable definition of fear as it relates to business and sometimes, it is healthy. Having a sense of fear is natural and can help keep us from jumping off the start line without a plan. A healthy amount of fear makes sure we complete our due diligence before deciding. Now, this will not relate to every decision being perfect, but it will keep us from make every decision on a whim.

You need to declutter the paralyzing fear, the fear that has you waking up at 2:00 AM in sweats, the fear that has you focusing on every story of business failure, the fear that keeps you locked in your house, staring at your bank account, and wondering why no one is coming to you. It has long been said animals can smell fear. Recently there is research that those with severe phobias emit an odor of fear in their sweat and how you project yourself when you are afraid. This is very interesting, and I have always said I noticed a downturn in my business when I am worrying too much {wait I thought you were talking about fear!}? I am, and it goes hand in hand with worry,

Definition of worry: to think about problems or fears: to feel or show fear and concern because you think that something bad has happened or could happen.

Worry is how I articulated my fears. I have been a worrywart for as long as I can remember. Looking back, I can now see it started in my unstable home. The worry when both my parents were home together and anticipating what would happen. Would they have another physical fight, or would there be calm in the house? Worry so consumed me it caused stomach problems for me. When I was working for a company, I didn't worry as much; I knew I was a great employee – given proper direction I could make anything work. I really didn't worry as much. When I took my first commission job, OH MY GOODNESS, worry manifested in the form of fear. It reared its big ugly head in a BIG way. Paralyzing me from any movement, I was not making sales, which is hard to do when you're not leaving the house. I over questioned every decision to the point of no decision, which is a decision. I was self-sabotaging, it was horrible. I did this on and off for months until I became single and the necessity for income became more significant than the fear. I got over my fear and worry quickly! I did a lot of talking to myself when worry crept back in, words of encouragement, positive phrases, etc. I still do this on a regular basis. This was all before I knew anything about the importance of what you say to yourself and who you surround yourself with.

Collectively, I've been working for myself for twelve years. I can tell you the number one self-sabotage for me is this one – fear & worry – it is junk I must declutter continually. When I notice a stall in my business, my introverted self- taking over, or just an everyday bad mood, I look first for clutter in my head. Thankfully, I am quick to notice, and it doesn't hold residence in my head as long as it used to.

Independence

This is my number two on the top list of stuff that clutters my mind. I remember the day of the week, where I was sitting, almost what I was wearing, when I received this as a bad review. I was a commission only sales person, and it was review time. I enjoyed review time because I typically received only high marks. When my review started out with all the positives I was glowing with pride. Then came the pause, we must talk about one thing, you need to ask for help, you are too independent.

WHAT? Too independent, how was this a bad thing? In the past, I have always been praised for my ingenuity, being a self-starter. My parents had it ingrained in me from as early as I can remember to be independent. I found myself completely stunned, wanting to defend myself, and all I could focus on was that one comment. How dare you tell me the way I have been surviving life all this time was negative. I politely smiled, said thank you for pointing that out, and promised I would ask for help more often. Yeah, not going to happen but I will tell you what you want to hear.

Admittedly, this is one of those items I know needs more work. It reveals its ugly head in my business and personal life regularly. I went on years before I took to heart that it's not necessarily being independent that is the problem, it's being so strongly independent that you shut others out. I have taken baby steps to deal with this. At the beginning when I would ask for help it went like this: "I could really use help with "xyz", but I completely understand if you can't. It would be nice, but I know you're busy so don't worry about it." If someone did say yes, they would help and for whatever reason not follow through, that reinforced why I never asked. It wasn't until recently when I had no choice but to ask for help, I experience blood clots in my leg and both lungs. This landed me in the hospital and then home on rest. Talk about a life lesson, when your mind says I got this I don't need help, and your body says, "Oh yeah really? How about we just make it really difficult to breathe." This was a great lesson in asking and accepting help. Luckily, I had friends who knew I would never ask and just did things like bringing me food and a fantastic husband who never complained about having to help, knowing full well it was one of the hardest things for me to do.

Typically, if you are too independent, it will show up in your business and your personal life. I know it's hard to ask for help, if you have been burned in the past. Take baby steps, ask for help by running a business idea past someone you trust, ask a client that loves you for a referral. Have a big trade show coming up, ask someone to hang out with you at your booth, the point is just ask. I can tell you it is uncomfortable; people aren't always going to do what they say they will. The times that help comes, makes it all worth it. Don't let your independence keep you from the next level in your business or your personal life.

I'm Right | One-Way:

This is funny, let me explain what I mean. This is not the long-running joke we have in my house where I am right so often it needs to be written on the calendar when I am wrong. I'm talking about the vision of the end result. We've spent all this time dreaming of our vision, creating every little detail, knowing without any doubt what the vision HAS to look like, and how we are achieving it. Sometimes this causes you to miss out on opportunities or keeps you from tweaking your vision even when it costs you success.

Being an entrepreneur requires flexibility and the ability to constantly tweak the course of your vision. If you get caught up in having one way to achieve your vision you can miss out on a lot of growth – both financially and personally. You may not see an offshoot of your current business that could lead to more customers. Let's face it you can't predict everything in owning a business; it's being flexible, analyzing how it's going, being open to suggestions, paying attention to what your customers are asking for, and asking for feedback. If you stay so focused on your original plan and only one way to achieve your vision, your road might be a little tough. I look back on my original business plan for Decluttered Spaces and must laugh. As a natural born organizer, I like everything in its place and planned out. I am also practical, what started out as my original vision has changed as the business has evolved. New offshoots have presented themselves which were not in the original plan.

Take the time every three months, find your happy place, and take the time to pause and look at your business. Are their tweaks that need to be made, are you at a juncture and need to explore another possible path? Just make sure you allow enough time to see if something is working or not. Find a trusted person or professional to help – a fresh set of eyes can be very enlightening.

Patience

What, business isn't going to happen overnight? I can't just nod my head, snap my fingers, turn on the now open sign and it happens overnight? It doesn't always work that way. I think sometimes we see someone else's success and think it happened overnight. I think we've all seen The Iceberg Illustration of business. People see the success, the tip of the iceberg, and don't realize what lies beneath the water; all the work, failures, sleepless nights, sacrifices, grit, and of course patience. And forget it if someone says, "Your so lucky, everything comes so easy for you." You politely smile while screaming on the inside, if you only knew what it took. Or they catch you on the day you school them on what it took – you're only human.

I hear it all the time; I didn't realize it was going to take this long, this is trying my patience, ugh can't it happen any quicker? I've said all of them. Just know, whether it's admitted or not, I don't care how patient a person you are. There will be moments where you are screaming for things to hurry up. Focus on the now, don't be wishing things to hurry up, causing you to miss out on the joy of the present. It will come when it comes, I know I dislike that phrase too, but it is true. Whatever your spiritual beliefs, opportunities are presented when you are ready to receive them.

Comparison

Comparison, the thief of joy and possibly why we are sometimes so impatient. Like I talked about with The Iceberg Analogy, comparison is very similar. We have that day where we want things to happen overnight? Why did it happen for her and not me, when is it my turn, my stuff it better than theirs? Oh, the nasty trap of comparison. One little scrap of comparison in our head is as destructible as a whole bag of impatience. Get rid of that immediately. If you must call that one trusted source, the one that knows all your clutter, vent for a minute and move right along. Comparison is easy to get caught up in, especially with social media. Let's be honest, we pretty much only see the FB of life. When you compare yourself to the perfect or the end result, you forget what it took to get there. The person isn't sharing everything that is going on in their life.

The other side of the comparison is; if I do my business like hers, I will copy that, I'll just borrow "xyz" word for word. This can happen slowly without you even realizing it. You compare your business with someone else that appears to be overwhelmingly successful and achieving the results you aren't, so you slowly become more like them. You forget about YOU, your voice, what makes you unique, whom you want to serve. You wake up and the business you started out loving, you don't. You forgot why you started it in the first place, and now nothing is working for you.

"To be yourself in a world that is constantly trying to make you something else is the greatest accomplishment." – Ralph Waldo Emerson

The only comparison you should do in business is numbers, last year's numbers to this years, last quarter to this quarter, etc. Comparing the numbers of your business – celebrate the successes and tweak when the numbers tell you to.

No!

You will hear it, and you will need to say it. I joke that owning your own business or working in commission sales is like online dating. You must put yourself out there knowing people are going to say no and you sometimes have to say no because you know it's not a good fit. My first venture into sales was working in a furniture store; it paid me $10 an hour or my commissions, whichever was higher. It gave me enough comfort with the $10/hour, which was way less after taxes and insurance, that I said, "I'm going to try this." It was honestly the best decision I made; it was my training ground for my future in entrepreneurship.

One of the best lessons was the word no. I would show people around the showroom, help them visualize their spaces, move pieces to the other side of the showroom to help them see what I saw, only to have them buy elsewhere. NO, after all I did? It was a hard lesson, but then I came to appreciate the no. They weren't saying no to me, they found a better-fit elsewhere, or their circumstances changed – the house sale didn't go through, they got transferred with a job, etc. It also taught me to listen; were these people serious shoppers or just enjoying some AC while dreaming of the changes they would like to make. Was I investing too much time in this one couple while ignoring the others that were buying? It was a great learning experience to step back and pay attention to my interactions with people and observe the professionals, the ones who were "lifers" as we called them. They could "read" a person with 95% accuracy, and their sales reflected it. These were great lessons to learn.

The other side of no is when to say it. Now in this situation I couldn't say to someone I don't want to be your sales person, I can tell by listening to you, you will be a pain in the butt and keep me from helping others. What I did quickly learn is if you have a timely break and hide out for a bit someone else will pick them up. This type of person wasn't going to say, "Nicole was helping me," they wanted an order taker. This was such a valuable lesson. So, how does that relate to owning a business? Sometimes you have to say no to that client that is sucking the life out of you, that one you thought, they must go. The person who wants to partner with you, but you get the icky feeling in your gut – that's your intuition screaming at you to say no. To all the freebies.

As an organizer, I get asked a lot to donate gift certificates, I would always say yes. After my medical event my energy was so precious, and while I never really said no when I was asked, I changed the amount of time. Have you heard of FOMO, fear of missing out? You might have to say no to some great networking, social activities, and kid's activities, to keep your sanity. When you find your calendar full of more of those FOMO activities, and not direct income-producing activities, it's time to exercise the word no. If you need a second person to run things buy, ask the friend that has no trouble telling you no, they will be honest and help you see why you need to say no.

Guilt/Shame/Regret/Failure

Now is not the time to exercise saying "NO" we are going there. This ugly clutter of Guilt ~ Shame ~ Regret ~ Failure. They intertwine themselves enhancing the feelings of each other. One of the worst culprits of mind clutter there is. SO much that my friend refuses to share her name but let me share her story. It's a bit long, but hey we are talking about the Viscous Four!

This is a story inspired by a dear friend of mine, whom I will call Victoria, and is dedicated to all of those, including myself, who sometimes live in regret of the past and wishing we could have a do-over. Unfortunately, or fortunately, there is no crystal ball to see into the future. We're fine that we don't have one when we are greeted with pleasant surprises but long for one when we must make a decision that has a big impact on our lives. We find ourselves at the end of a life chapter that didn't go nearly as well as we planned. We have all been there, all experienced times in our life we wish we could change, and all have that secret list of what we should have done differently. It's what we do with that secret list that is so important in the future decisions we make. Do you hold onto that list, not just the experiences, but also the feelings the experiences left you with? Being a failure, guilt, shame, regret. Confirming words spoken to you in the past, feeling like you will never succeed. To the outsider, you appear so resilient, meanwhile inside you're feeling defeated. While each experience on the secret list by itself is small, all of them added together can become a weight that will hold you down if you realize it or not.

I have known Victoria for about four years now; when we first met, she was embarking on a new chapter of her business life, being the proud owner of a franchise. She did her due diligence in researching this franchise, besides being in an industry that was very lucrative and a much-needed service in our area, it also fed her passion. Her passion for helping a segment of our population that was often ignored, preyed upon, and not treated the way they should be. This was a win-win all the way around. We met because our businesses were an immediate strategic partnership. Upon our first and second meeting, we realized not only were our businesses a strategic partnership, but we also were a lot alike and became fast friends. Fast friends didn't come immediately with opening up – we both are private people. Over time her business grew, she was making great connections, helping lots of people but it was all coming at a cost.

There are pros and cons to owning a franchise, and in this case, the cons were outweighing the pros. The franchisor didn't disclose the financials truthfully, the projections Victoria was led to believe would occur were not. The business she was in was much needed BUT also had a fair bit of competition. The competition was not only for customers, it was the employees too. One of the most significant complaints I hear amongst people I know who run companies with employees is the lack of loyalty; I know in most cases companies don't show devotion either. Victoria had employees leaving her to work for the competition over 50 cents – they would be offered 50 cents more and hour and jump ship. Consider the cost it took for Victoria to hire them, each of them having to be background checked and drug screened. Victoria found much of her time with the HR hat on, and less time doing what she loved, helping her clients. She also found out that the franchisor was very rigid about the business model, especially when it came to social media marketing. Website changes took forever and when she offered to do things herself they didn't want to give up control. The support she was receiving and what she was promised were not what was agreed upon. Had Victoria had a crystal ball, this is a venture she would have never done. The amount of money taken to start this business, the fees and overhead to keep it going, and not seeing where there would be any return in the immediate future led to a

TOUGH decision. Upon the annual review – a tough conversation with her and her husband ended in the decision to sell her franchise and stop the financial "bleed."

Now while my friend will not admit it verbally, this left her feeling like a failure, regretting she ever started that venture. For her, this seemed like she had made a rash decision to sink a good portion of the family's savings into a business she couldn't make successful. While anyone that knows her saw her working her butt off. Knew she was doing everything she could to make it succeed, and me knowing the other information, I could see it was nothing she did wrong, and she didn't have a choice – it was better to get out and take the loss, it was only going to get worse. I looked at her decision and saw victory; a lot of people would ignore the financial drain and keep playing "poker" hoping to hit the elusive jackpot. It takes a lot of strength to have that tough conversation with your spouse who has been supporting you all along and say I don't think it's going to work. This was a hit financially and emotionally that would have taken the weakest out but not Victoria. She took the lessons she had learned, the favorite part of the business, and the connections she had made and created a new business. I remember where we met when we first talked about it, I LOVED the idea and I felt so strongly this was going to be an excellent fit for her and a much-needed service. And here goes Round 2, which felt like round 10 of a boxing match.

Victoria's next venture started – transitioning straight out of the franchise to her own business. Unfortunately, like most of us, there wasn't the time to regroup mentally, she had to keep moving without missing a beat; business name, website, business cards, and then contacting all her connections with the exciting news. And explain the transition – I remember the conversation about how I am going to explain things. I could tell she felt like I think a lot of us would – I failed and what are people going to think. While her new business was well received it was more of a consultative business, and as any of us who have been in this sort of business you find people who want to get the free info but not pay, and when you have a giving heart, it's effortless to share for free. The sales process was slow, there was a lot of education to help people understand, and Victoria had already "fought" ten rounds. And her business, like my organizing business, was one of those that people wanted but didn't always want to pay for and they just had to be fed up doing it on their own before they would hire you.

I watched Victoria keep working away, meanwhile dealing with significant health issues with one of her family members. She shared none of the personal stuff that was going on. I would always tell her that's a great story, it ties in with your business, you need to share your story. Since by now we were basically sisters, she would give me that sisterly "love" and tell me where to put my ideas. I could see her fight fading, she was tired, like we all get when you just feel you are spinning your wheels and getting nowhere. She was putting pressure on herself that was unrealistic. It did not surprise me when she told me she was submitting applications to companies. Like a lot of us our commitment to family must come into play. She had an internal commitment to help be a contributing financial provider for her family. To replenish the nest egg, she "depleted." This was not a pressure put on by her husband – this was an internal pressure. With perfectionism its sometimes easier to see what went wrong versus what went right. Part of me was sad that she was applying for other companies, but I also knew there was a strength and wisdom to her decision. I knew she had to do this for her family, I could see she needed a break. And I knew whoever hired her would be beyond fortunate to have her. That is what Victoria needed right now, she needed to be working and not spinning her wheels. She needed to bring in "steady" income – she was smart though she knew her value and was hired on with a company that paid salary plus commissions – no limiting her ability to kick butt.

You may ask yourself why are you telling this story of "Victoria"? There are valuable lessons to be learned, while my friend sometimes sees herself as not succeeding, I see her as VICTORIOUS, hence the fake name Victoria. Entrepreneurs don't always know when to walk away, don't have the strength to have to tough conversations with those they love, aren't able to pivot their lessons into something else, and sometimes pivot again. From my perspective, we have all experienced some Victoria in our life. And while my friend still has not burned that secret list she holds too close to her chest you would never know based on her stoic front and how she is kicking butt in her new venture. I have the honor and privilege of a small glimpse of her life she still doesn't share it all, but I knew her story had to be told. For those who have made large investments not to have them work out, for those who feel they can't take one more round in "fighting" for your business to succeed – it's okay to step out and get a J.O.B. for a bit – there is no shame in that. Stay true to yourself, give yourself grace, and refuel/renew your mind and soul. Easier said than done - this is the adventure of the business owner.? Know when changes need to be made but don't be harder on yourself then you would be to a "sister" you like.

Know guilt, shame, regret, and failure do not serve you in your business life or your personal life. This is something I battled with for years; it wasn't until I participated in a personal growth program that I could fully understand what I was experiencing and how it was hindering joy in my life. I still experience the feelings of failure, but now at least I can recognize it and address it before it opens the door for regret, shame, and guilt. Please know if this is clutter you hold onto, it may not clear out overnight. You might think you have it all and then an experience, like opening that closet door, reveals more decluttering to do. Be patient and loving to yourself. Keep improving every day in a small way, baby steps!

Love YOU

Yes, love you!! Speaking from my own experience, and a lot of my clients, sometimes we are our own worst enemies. We critique ourselves the hardest, we say things to ourselves internally that we would never say to someone we like let alone someone we love. Why are you saying it to you? I mentioned earlier I talk to myself a lot and I didn't realize how important it was to surround myself with supportive, positive people. I strongly disliked me for the longest time. I would have people tell me how confident I was, how I had it all together, I was so organized, etc. Meanwhile to everyone compliment they had for me, I had five things I was doing wrong and needed to improve. I learned very early to receive that compliment and say thank you. However, it took a while to accept that compliment and mean it when I said thank you. So now I talk to myself a lot, I tell myself I am fabulously awesome, start my day with gratitude, and when I feel the self-hatred train coming on I turn to an inspirational podcast and turn off all social media, that only fuels my self-hatred.

Being around positive, supportive people is a MUST for me, my Tribe of Wave Makers. I am keenly aware now of the fuel negative people, gossip, getting wrapped up in comparison, that allows my self-hatred to grow out of control. Now I don't always like me, I still am too hard on myself but for the most part, I love me. Now I didn't say I was perfect, I said I love me and that means I get to like the parts of me that I don't like. But instead of focusing on the things about me I don't like I focus on what I love and work on the little things that need to change for myself. For lots of people, self- hatred is easy to hide but it will show up in your business and personal life in little ways that can lead to a very destructive end.

Next time you are mean to you – picture a child, a dog, your best friend, whomever that person is – if you would not say those words to them you should NOT being saying them to you. If this is your clutter, practice saying something kind to yourself every day, receiving compliments given, and as corny as it sounds post positive sayings around your home, your car, your office, etc. It helps. And in severe cases please seek professional help; there is no shame in that.

I could go on and on with client stories, the other thoughts and feelings that need to be Decluttered – how about perfectionism or lack of confidence? If you take anything away, stop and listen to what is fueling your beliefs and actions, what negativity do you need to declutter from your mind/thoughts. Those things that steal your joy and keep you from living the life you desire both professionally and personally. Don't look at the clutter in your life as only the tangible – it all starts with the intangible.

NICOLE LYNN

Nicole Lynn is one of those naturally born organizers - her own mother describes her as "always needing order" and yes, she does feel a label maker is a great birthday present. After 20 years of working in corporate America, Nicole decided to do what gives her the most joy: organizing spaces for people that bring harmony to their worlds. Nicole used to spend her Friday nights helping her friends with bathroom drawers, kitchen shelves, and shoes - she now brings her expertise to your life and spaces.

Nicole Lynn started Decluttered Spaces in 2013 to help people organize their homes and offices, thereby living happier lives with less stress. Today, Nicole creates simplified internal systems, offers training classes for small businesses, and consults in a private, online community {check out AWaveMaker.com}. Oh, yes. She still organizes on-site for clients, rolls up her sleeves, and gets things in order.

Nicole has what it takes to bring your spaces to the next level. She believes firmly in creating spaces that work for you and not for her. This belief is imperative to create harmony in your spaces. Let Nicole, your Harmonizing Specialist, change the way you use your space and make it a place you want to be.

Nicole Lynn is a National Award-Winning Speaker on the topic of Domestic Violence and the impact it has on children, was awarded the prestigious Frisco Texas Chamber of Commerce Solopreneur of the Year for 2015 as well as finalist for Entrepreneur of the Year 2016 and 2017. She serves on a select committee of WEB, Women Enhancing Business and always encourages her clients to support local charities through donations of items when possible.

Nicole doesn't believe she is an author although she is the best-selling author of the Decluttering Your Life Series, contributing author of best seller Behind Her Brand Entrepreneur Edition Vol 5, adult coloring/journal book Dreams Need Wings, and now compiler and author of this book. Nicole has also started a personal blog Life by Grace vulnerably sharing the life stories that have made her the woman she is today, www.LifeByGrace.org

- www.DeclutteredSpaces.com
- www.AWaveMaker.com
- https://www.facebook.com/PiperTheFlyingPig/
- https://www.instagram.com/decluttered_spaces/
- https://www.linkedin.com/in/nicolelynnsc/

.

SHEA KRAMER, DC
The Power of Intention

The power of intention is the power to manifest, to create, to live a life of unlimited abundance, and to attract into your life the right people at the right moments. - The Power of Intention by Wayne Dyer

This quote changed the trajectory of my life. I was a young 18-year-old girl, living in a college dorm contemplating what I wanted to do with my life. I had decided at age 11 that becoming a chiropractor was my life goal- but doubt and insecurity got in my way of judgement upon applying for college. Instead of packing up my life at age 18 to move to Atlanta Georgia to pursue my dream, I started college at Ohio University for my freshman year. Reading the book titled "The Power of Intention" lead to a series of events that left me 100% positive that pursuing my childhood dream was my calling.

I grew up in a very modest home in small town, Ohio. My dad was the hardest working blue-collar worker out there, and my mom was fully committed to raising my brother and I in the most loving way possible. I was very blessed to be surrounded by family who supported me and guided me to have an enjoyable childhood. But their sacrifices did not go unnoticed.... I knew that my dad would work overtime whenever possible to provide for our family and that my mother would give the shirt off her back if it meant me or my brother getting what we needed or wanted. I learned the lesson of being selfless from these experiences. This lesson has been very applicable in my entrepreneurship- learning to be selfless for the sake of growth and legacy during a society that prefers instant gratification.

Growing up in a small town where you are the fifth generation of your family also meant that everybody was watching, and it was hard to get away with anything. For me, it was never the fear of getting caught- but the fear of being a disappointment to those who were important to me, almost to a fault. I remember my mom finding an old piece of homework I crumbled up and threw under the bed when I was in third grade because I got a C on it, and I was devastated. The truth was that she did not care what grades I got, just that I did my best. In fact, I never got disciplined because of my performance in school but the pressure I put on myself surpassed any discipline my parents would have provided. My mother constantly voiced her confidence in me, and how proud she was of things I accomplished. Nevertheless, being strict on the standards I set for myself was a habit I started very early and has continued to be one of my best and worst attributes. Even into my adulthood, this has both helped and hindered me.

One of the biggest influences during my childhood was my uncle, my moms' brother. He introduced my family to (what seemed like magic) chiropractic, was committed and stubborn about the goals he set, and helped lead me to my profession. Growing up, my brother and I were your all-too-common "sick" kids. Always on antibiotics for something. Can we just talk about how terrible amoxicillin tastes?!? I have nightmares to this day about that thick pink sweet potion. But I jokingly talk about how every night with dinner we would have our meal, our glass of sweet tea, and our daily dose of amoxicillin. There was even one time that a new liquid medication was thrown into the mix- and because I was hostile toward medicine at this point, they lied and told me it was "coke syrup". You know your family roots run deep in the south of Georgia when you pretend to like something terrible is supposed to taste like Coca-Cola. But we each had our own plague- for my brother, it was ear infections and for me it was strep throat. In fact, the year my brother was four, he had eight ear infections in a row. Our sweet pediatrician finally said it was time to stop the madness and that my brother needed surgery to put tubes in his ears to help them drain. My parents, wanting to do whatever it took to help him, scheduled him for that surgery. At this point in time, my uncle was away at college and studying chiropractic, something we were very unfamiliar with. He mentioned to my mom that chiropractic might be able to help his ear infections. Chiropractic?? Ear infections?? Isn't chiropractic something you do for neck pain, back pain, and maybe after a car accident? Not for four-year old's who have terrible immune systems. But since my mom trusted her brother's judgement, off we went to the local chiropractor. This was our first experience with the magic of chiropractic. I watched chiropractic bring life back to my brother's immune system. I saw him improve almost immediately from his plague of ear infections. In fact, he did so well with chiropractic care that he no longer needed that surgery he was scheduled for. My first lesson in natural healing started here in my childhood. I knew this was what I needed to do with my life- share the magic of chiropractic with others.

I started my freshman year of college at Ohio University, taking as many credit hours during the first quarter they would allow. This put me in a little over my head because I had yet to experience a difficult college course. Until this time, I had an easy time with academics and excelling in my grades. But those early mornings in physics class with 100+ of my fellow freshman had me questioning if I could even make it through that first quarter. This was a wakeup call I needed to step up my game and re-evaluate my strategy to succeed. I quickly realized that the high standards and expectations I had set for myself up until this point would need to become more flexible. Maybe my mom was right- I needed to do the best I could. That perfectionist voice in my head hated having to even entertain this conversation. Experiencing this little wake-up call, that the fear of doing badly was not good enough to maintain successful outcomes, served as a lesson that I could reference many times in the upcoming years.

During my first quarter of college, I read a book titled "The Power of Intention" by Dr. Wayne Dyer. This was my first introduction to anything about the law of attraction and how you can influence and shape your own world with your thoughts. Reading about these principles gave me a new excitement for life and for my future. At age eighteen I understood that controlling my own thought process could mold my future. I did not know that the lessons I picked up in this reading would coincide with major life decisions. During this time, I was also pondering my future in chiropractic. I could have gone straight to Atlanta to start my undergraduate studies instead of going to Ohio University, but a small feeling of doubt creeped into my head my senior year of high school. I was worried (imagine that) that I would get to Atlanta and fail or be unhappy with my choice, and then stuck in a state 500 miles away from home. But I couldn't help but to sit in my freshman dorm and think "what if". I was attending school at a great university, making wonderful new friends, exploring new sports and experiences, but felt somewhat unfulfilled because I could not think of anything else I wanted to pursue career-wise except for chiropractic, which was not an available degree at Ohio University. I began searching through the website for the chiropractic school I was interested in and submitted my dorm address for an information packet to learn more about the school. A few days later, I received a phone call from an advisor from that chiropractic school. He cheerfully introduced himself and said that he was very excited that I was applying for Life University. Wait, what? I was so confused. I had simply requested an information booklet from the school and he called that day in expectation that I was applying. I thought….is this the power of intention showing itself to me already? The gentleman told me that my application should be in my mailbox within 6-8 weeks. About two weeks after that conversation, my uncle drove over to Ohio University for a weekend to check out the campus and see how I was doing. We went to dinner, talked about school, chiropractic, and life in general. I didn't even bring up my conversation with the advisor from Life University because it had slipped my mind. As he was preparing to leave and go back to our hometown, I checked my mailbox before we walked out. Low and behold, a giant packet of paperwork was waiting on me. It was an application for Life University, the chiropractic school I wanted to attend. Four weeks earlier than I expected it. My uncle's alma mater. The profession that the person who came to visit me that day at Ohio University introduced me to. Now, this was the power of intention at its finest.

My first phone call the next day was to my mother. I asked her if she believed God closes certain doors and opens others for a reason, because I felt resistance at my current school and saw opportunity at Life University. After experiencing what I thought was the power of intention, on top of feeling like my purpose was not fulfilled at Ohio University, I felt like maybe God was tapping me on the shoulder saying that I needed to change. I told her what happened and that I felt like it was time for me to make the move. I was ready to leave my Ohio roots and head down to the Peach State to chase my dream of becoming a chiropractor. Sometimes I can't believe that she was ok with me moving 500 miles away to a big city that I was unfamiliar with, especially not knowing a single person in the area. That was the thing about my mom though- she always supported my decisions no matter how big, small, conservative or lofty they may be. She would always say "you are destined for greatness", and that provision held a small but mighty space in my mind. At nineteen, I was headed southbound with a U-Haul full of my belongings and a few family members to help me set up my new life.

I had to grow up fast in that first year of living on my own. I relied on faith, grace, and more coffee than any one person should consume. I quickly realized that while I was successful in academics until this point in life, I did not excel in common sense. Case in point, I almost got evicted in my first thirty days of living alone. You see, up until this point I had always lived with my parents or in a dorm. I had never needed to pay rent, be mindful of bill due dates, or a plethora of other "adult" responsibilities. Why don't they teach life skills more in high school??! Well anyway, less than 3 weeks after moving into my new apartment, I had a nice little eviction notice on my door. I must have looked like a deer in the headlights when I saw that. Embarrassment kicked in hardcore. What on earth am I getting evicted for?!? Well as it turns out, it turned out that rent is due on the FIRST of the month...not according to the date you moved in. How did I not know this? I can laugh about this looking back, but I can assure you there was no laughing when it happened. In fact, there were tears. Lots of tears. Boo-hoo crying while driving to class, ashamed of common sense that I did not have and wallowing in a major self-pity party. That is when a car pulled out in front of me and through my tear stained sunglasses, I read the license plate on this vehicle.... "UROK". I took my sunglasses off, wiped my eyes and re-focused on the letters to make sure I was reading correctly. I thought this is surely God showing himself to me. I submitted my rent payment with an apology, dried my tears, and learned that even I was deserving of a little grace.

Chiropractic school was transformational for me. Starting graduate level classes at the age of 19 left me with stress and anxiety

I did not know how to cope with. My main strategy was internalizing, crying, or complaining to my mother I could not get through this. Regardless of my poor strategies, I was bullheaded about conquering school. I set a goal to graduate as a Doctor of Chiropractic by the age of 23. There was nothing that could stand in my way and I will do whatever it took. Multiple coffee shop employees knew me by my first name...this included Starbucks, Dunkin Donuts, and even Krispy Kreme. For some reason I loved the coffee at Krispy Kreme. There is a little humor to that I will share later.

Every quarter in chiropractic school was a ten-week sprint. At the end of each sprint, we would have 1-2 weeks filled with exam after exam, sometimes up to twelve total. I remember those exam weeks and how we would have to walk single file, nothing in our hands except a pencil and ID, filter into a giant room and have an hour or so to complete the test. As stressful as this may seem, part of me thrived on these test weeks. Something about filling out the bubbles on those scantrons to answer questions I was confident in knowing made me feel very accomplished. Also, knowing that at the end of that week I could declare victory on another quarter. Ten weeks closer to my goal. Little did I know, the hardest part would be yet to come, after graduation.

The experiences I had living in Atlanta weren't just about the education I received, but about understanding who I was as a person and who I wanted to be. I was blessed with a group of girlfriends who became my tribe, and to this day are still some of my best friends. We became each other's second family. I learned the importance of community and how essential it is to have people to depend on and to also be a dependable person myself. Time with these girls became a resting place for me- an escape from the hustle and bustle of school. We had "family" dinners, went on road trips together, and explored the city of Atlanta. During developing our professional lives, we established lifelong companionship and friendship. We all shared chiropractic school in common, so it was easy to vent about what was going on to someone who understood and could give advice or just be a listening ear. I believe in investing in your friendships. I once read a quote that said, "Relationships are the currency of life", and this had a profound effect on me. As cliché as it sounds, a lesson from this period in my life would be "find your tribe and love them hard".

One of the best things that happened to me during my grad school years was meeting my future husband. Who knew that a friend-of-a-friends roommate from Seattle who happened to show up at my apartment pool one day would be my life partner. It turned out that this guy moved to Atlanta to pursue chiropractic as well, and just so happened to be in my class. The graduate program for chiropractic is much like grade school in the sense that you are in the same classes with the same people all day every day for the duration of the program. When I arrived at our first class of the quarter, I was excited to see that someone I had met before starting the program was in my class. We did not speak much at first, but because he was the roommate of a friend of mine, we always ended up at the same get togethers on the weekends. Before I knew it, he became my standing study date. We would spend hours at Panera (again- their coffee was delicious) studying for our classes. The study dates got longer and longer and before I knew it, there was more leisure conversation than there was studying. For a long time, I was in denial that this was the beginning of our love story. The study dates turned into real dates, and then real vacations, and then real meet-the-family trips. We spent the next couple of years learning about each other, dating, traveling, and deciding that we would commit to spending the rest of our lives together. Oh, and be in business together, too. Yep- we were taking our status of being together all day every day during class to being together all day every day together in business. He brought a calmness to my crazy, a serenity to my anxiety and adventure to my routine. There has always been an element of spontaneity in my relationship with him, which is one of my favorite things about our relationship. Sometimes that would mean a long conversation over a glass of whiskey (another love we shared) and sometimes that meant upgrading to first class on a vacation to Jamaica that he won on a raffle. The vacation I left the vouchers (pre-iPhone days, y'all) at home sitting on the desk and it didn't cross my mind until we were taxiing down the runway. Cue the whiskey, flight attendant! (Full disclosure, the Jamaican hotel was more than accommodating to my forgetful ways, and we enjoyed a wonderful authentic Jamaican vacation). Jason proposed to me three months before graduation, and this spurred some of the quickest and most influential decisions of my life.

Remember the stubborn and bullheaded traits I mentioned about myself before? I really let them show during the process of deciding what was next for me and Jason. My five-year plan past graduating from chiropractic school included what I thought was most important to me- moving to the beach in Florida. I could not fathom or understand why my Seattle-ite fiancé was opposed to this, and why he was dead set on moving back to Seattle. I mean, who would choose the rainy pacific northwest over a hot sunny beach in Florida?!?! You can imagine there were some serious disagreements during this time. I was vocal and rude to him about how I would not even consider Seattle. He politely shared with me that Florida was not an option. The worst part about it was that we were on a time crunch and needed to move somewhere new to establish our business within six months of getting engaged. That sounds like a real engagement-honeymoon period, no?! Our decision took multiple trips to different cities, contemplating what was important to each of us, and setting our egos aside. Not easy. There was one trip to Texas that we planned to kill 2 birds with one stone- a wedding in San Antonio and a drive through Houston to see if that would be our next spot. However, the trip started in Dallas because we had friends there we wanted to visit. We spent a short few days there, met my friend's business partner, and got pitched the idea of moving to Dallas. Our first thought was heck no, the main purpose of the entire Texas trip was to explore Houston, not Dallas. Do not mess with our plans sir. We are moving forward.

Well, the short Dallas stay turned into visiting friends in Austin, attending a wedding in San Antonio, and ultimately visiting the town on our list of potential living spots, Houston Texas. Only, every sign pointed to NO. The second we landed in Dallas, person after person told us that Houston was a terrible idea. We shunned their negativity and continued our way. Upon entering Houston, we found the community we had researched on the world wide web and stumbled upon a vacant space for business lease. We excitingly gave the landlord a phone call, who returned our enthusiasm with more information on the space. Her next question was, "What type of business will you open in this space?". When we answered with our plans of opening a chiropractic business, her enthusiasm went awry. "Oh, I am sorry," she said, "my nephew is graduating from chiropractic school this year and he will be the chiropractor of this town". Stomach dropped. Morale dropped. A mutual glance that read "what's next" was shared between me and Jason. We drove back to the hotel and had a long conversation about what this meant. I have always been dependent upon my gut feeling in life. I feel like the more in-tune you are with your gut feeling, the better it will serve you. I have always tried my best to be hyper-aware of what my inner voice was saying, and it was saying that Houston was a definite no. I shared this with Jason and he agreed. Unfortunately for us, Houston was the last spot on our list that we were considering. What would we do now?! Every place we had visited on our list p until this point had proven itself wrong for us. I asked Jason, should we consider the offer from the business partner of my friend? Could Dallas be an option? There was a long pause before either of us interjected a comment on that question. Dallas was a great city, we had a great offer, but it just didn't offer the things we were looking for. We wanted an outdoor city, whether that mean beach or mountains. Dallas has neither. But for some reason we felt the need to explore this option more. Maybe it was the time crunch, maybe it was a whisper from God, or maybe it was just the exhaustion from not being able to plan until this point. We decided that evening that we would give Dallas a shot. The next morning, we called a real estate agent and said, "we need a place to stay, and we will be there in 3 weeks". Talk about a shotgun decision. It was Steve Jobs who said "You can't connect the dots looking forward; you can only connect them looking backwards. So, trust that the dots will somehow connect in your future." This quote could not be more applicable to the experience we have had since deciding to move to Dallas up until our seventh year here. We traveled back to Atlanta that weekend and packed up our belongings for our westbound life expansion.

As it turns out, nothing can quite prepare you for the life transformation that happens when you start a business from scratch right out of school where they teach absolutely no business sense. We were the greenest of green in getting started, negotiating our own building space and developing our own marketing plans. We started out full of vigor and eagerness for this baby of ours,

Revolution Chiropractic. We joined the chamber, our nearest BNI group, and even walked door-to-door in 110-degree weather telling people that this would be the best chiropractic office yet. We relied on skills we learned from serving other chiropractic offices during school, which included tenacity and resilience. Every no put us one step closer to a yes. Every hardship was nothing more than a lesson in disguise. We worked day after day, hour after hour, to make sure our dream of establishing a successful business was a reality. I can happily say in 2018, we have fulfilled that dream of ours.

Building Revolution Chiropractic into what is today has not been a walk in the park, but it is a park that I am forever grateful to have walked through. In the early years of our business, I had a very difficult time dealing with the anxiety and worry habits that I had developed very early in life. I had to learn that success does not care about your anxiety. In fact, those tactics will earn you a fast pass to failing rather than succeeding. There has been and honestly always will be a learning curve in this for me- because each level of success brings its own trial and errors. Our high energy, in the beginning, built amazing momentum but momentum that is not sustained declines quickly. Our first year included multiple attempts at building and sustaining that momentum while also trying to find balance working hard and not getting burnt out. The fact that we were living in a city that we had no connections or family in further reinforced that difficulty. By the grace of God, another couple we knew from our time in Atlanta also moved to Dallas. They became our new community and our best friends. The four of us have established our roots here in this city and we have shared incredible memories together, including a standing Friday date at our favorite drink spot to hash out the troubles of our week and how we would tackle them in the next. The lessons I learned in chiropractic school proved to still be true- that community is so important, and relationships are worth every second you invest into them.

I will never forget one day early in practice- a patient that we had been seeing for a few weeks approached me in the office and whispered that he needed to talk. He explained how he and his (ex) wife had worked together for a long period and how is it was the worst idea ever- and that we should professionally separate before it gets hard. At first, I was irritated, but then I felt bad for him that it did not work well for him. I knew I needed to commit to maintaining a sense of grace for my future husband and me, that the story would be different for us. Over time I have learned that this is an evolving pursuit, each year is different than the previous and that tweaking how we act or react is necessary from time to time. We rely on our faith and our commitment to each other with an element of grace and a few doses of whiskey to get us through difficult times. Although you never know what the future may hold, we have been successful in our efforts for ten years now. I hear that ten years of experience validates you as an expert in anything, so I say with humor that we are experts in surviving life and business together.

Growing from an eager 18-year-old excited for my future to a 31-year-old business owner has been filled with lessons. I set out to accomplish the goal of graduating as Doctor of Chiropractic at age 23- and I crushed that goal. Though there were difficulties in achieving that, it did not quite prepare me for the marathon of opening and running a business at that young age. Hindsight tells me that taking a little more time in those younger years would have allowed for more emotional-health growth, but I believe everything happens for a reason. Maybe that reason was so I could meet my future husband or maybe that reason was so that I could tell my story and inspire someone in the next generation of women. Nonetheless,

I am eternally grateful for all the highs and all the lows that have gotten me to this point. The bitterness of failed attempts makes the honey of success taste so much sweeter. I like to think I have left a little mark each place I have gone. I proved this to myself on a trip to Atlanta, 5 years after graduating. I drove past that Krispy Kreme and remembered how good that coffee had tasted, so I went through the drive through to get myself one. The gentleman in the window said to me, "hey, aren't you that girl who used to drive through here in a red S-10 truck?" We shared a mutual laugh and I thought to myself, how sweet is it to experience so much change yet somehow still be the same.

My hope for those reading my story is that you will finish feeling refreshed. That your principles are worth holding onto, that you can forge change and remain true to yourself, and that success is possible if you are committed to it. I have found through my years that the key to success is persevering and constantly picking yourself and others up. You have a gift that you may or may not be aware of right now- but it is there and waiting to be shared with the world. For myself, I think those gifts are the magic of chiropractic, the strong will of being committed to my goals, and the awareness that my (and your) tribe is one of the most important things in life. God is intertwined in all the details and if you forget to see forest for the trees, you might miss out on the subtle hints he shares. Be strong, courageous, and always remember... "UROK".

SHEA KRAMER, DC

Dr. Shea Kramer grew up in a small town in southwest Ohio, where she took an interest in natural health and healing at a very young age. After witnessing her brother's health drastically improve under chiropractic care, she decided at age 11 that she wanted to be a Doctor of Chiropractic. She spent her middle school and high school years focused on learning more about the profession and preparing for chiropractic school.

At the age of 19 she moved to Atlanta Georgia to attend Life University, a prestigious and nationally recognized Doctor of Chiropractic program. Her commitment to goals and determination to succeed led her to graduate as a Doctor of Chiropractic at age 23. She met her now husband while living in Atlanta.

Dr Shea and her husband moved to Dallas Texas in 2011 to pursue entrepreneurship and open their own business, Revolution Chiropractic. They have become an established center for chiropractic excellence.

Together, they are members of Genesis Metro Church. They also make charitable contributions to Connect Global, a ministry focused on providing sustainable solutions. Locally, they give back to This Side UP! Family Center, to help move families from surviving to thriving.

.

- www.facebook.com/RevolutionChiro
- Instagram- Revolution_Chiropractic__Dallas

CINDY BALSLEY

Growing up with three siblings, I observed the dichotomy of a typical American household in the mid-to-late twentieth century. My father had a full-blown career, while my mother was expected to be the perfect homemaker. She had to take care of all four of us, cook meals every day and keep a tidy home. There was never a day I didn't appreciate my parents' sacrifices, but the more I grew up, the more I realized how uninterested I was in playing the "traditional" female role. Of course, I wanted to be a wife and mother, but I wanted a career too. My father saw these aspirations as nothing more than daydreams. In my house, it was implied that my sister and I's central goal should be to find a husband, settle down and stay at home while the man in our life pursued an admirable career. I was young, but I was determined. My father's outdated views and opinions did not sit well with me. My plan to seek success in a male-dominated corporate world was a common topic of debate between us.

In1983, I left Houston to pursue a career in Dallas. Without support or direction from my parents, who urged me to forgo a career in favor of marriage, I wanted a fresh start and found myself with a job in insurance. As I got increasingly familiar with my field, I fell into a pattern of moving around to several different companies. One day I realized why I hadn't felt inclined to dedicate myself to a single employer; I was making money for *other* people. Instead of building up success in the name of a corporation, I wanted to build success for myself.

As many people know, starting your own company from the ground up is far from simple. I had asked around about companies that would let me build my book of business when I ended up landing an interview with one that we'll call "Company A." Company A was a small, local Property & Casualty insurance company. Keep in mind this was back in the day when insurance agents were 95% male and only 5% female. The one thing I'll never forget from my first encounter with this company was when the interviewer asked me if I could do the job "as well as a man" to which I responded, "No, I can do it better." During my search for a parent company, I had asked my father to lend me $5,000 to help me get my new business off the ground. Disappointingly, he said no. He did not have any confidence in my abilities to success in a male-dominated business environment. Rather than let my father's lack of support get the best of me, I persevered. I gathered the necessary funds through my own determination and some help from close friends and a few prior bosses.

Company A was a definitive point in my career. It was a good learning experience, and I found out that running your own show sounds a lot more glamorous than it is. Suddenly, you're responsible for everything: sales, lack of sales, marketing, taxes, human resources, office supplies, phone expenses and more. This new undertaking was overwhelming, but I was able to reduce a portion of my business expenses by working from home. This allowed me to experience the reality of running my own business but taking time away from a typical office environment was a weight off my shoulders. My time with Company A lasted about three years. Just as I was building a good-sized book of business, a slew of hailstorms left the small corporation with unmanageable expenses and Company A went bankrupt.

After my time with Company A, I could not bear the thought of stepping back and working for someone else. Once again, I hit the pavement and ended up with a major direct writer; let's call them "Company B." I was fortunate in that I was able to roll over a good number of my clients from Company A to Company B. Despite another new start, my confidence did not waver. Honestly, being single during this time in my life was a huge relief. I felt like even if my business endeavors didn't work out, I would only risk my own financial security, rather than that of an entire family. I fell in love with Company B. I was so happy with work. Around the same time, I found the love of my life and got married. My business was going so well that my husband ended up joining me in the office. Not only was I satisfied with myself, but I also knew I had "made it" in the industry.

One of the biggest lessons I've had to learn time and time again is that life happens, even if you own a business. You always must deal with life and your business at the same time. It's not like you can take sick leave or extended personal time when you're in charge of everything. On the surface, it looked like I was living the perfect life, but things are not always as they seem. In 1995, after a bout of infertility, I finally got pregnant. I never seem to do things the "normal" or "easy" way. My pregnancy was rough. I had morning sickness morning, noon and night, right from the start. My husband worked with me about a year before my pregnancy, and since we were commuting to the same place, he could drive me to work while I carried my trusty puke bucket along with us. The Bucket went with me everywhere I went. There was no way I could stay home, I had to work, and having a bucket with me all the time was the key factor to my success. I started interviews for an assistant, but just when I found the perfect candidate, I had even more pregnancy complications had to go on complete bed rest. My husband would set a cooler of drinks and food by the bed for snacks for the day, as I could not get out of bed except to use the restroom. To say this time was frustrating is putting it mildly. I still took some calls and did some work from bed. When I was finally able to return to the office, I was ready to dive in with my new assistant. I thought I would have at least a few months to train her, but life was about to take over again.

After work one night I started having contractions, but the baby wasn't due for seven or eight more weeks. I went to the hospital and was given medication to stop my early labor. The medication worked, and labor stopped, but one of the rare side effects of the medication was fluid build-up in the lungs. Of course, I was one of the few people affected. I couldn't breathe and was placed in the ICU until a group of doctors could figure out what to do with me. And remember, I still had a business to run. The doctor said my organs were starting to fail, so I was put on a ventilator. I don't remember any part of the delivery. God took care of it all, like He always does. I woke up the day after delivery, still on the ventilator. I had to write questions out since I couldn't talk. My husband Kirk and I had decided not to find out the baby's sex beforehand, so this note-writing system is how I found out we had a baby girl; we decided to name her Audra. I had to wait three days before I could see her. The nurses would send pictures up to my room until I was able to go visit the NICU myself. I was able to go home after just a few days, but Audra had to stay in the hospital for over a week.

With all this chaos going on, I *still* had a business to run. Customers don't want to hear excuses about your personal issues, they want you to solve their problems and answer their questions. Eight weeks after delivery, I returned to work. It was weird coming back and settling in; I guess because so much happened while I was gone. Before Audra was born, we decided Kirk would say home with her while I returned to work. I felt like things were back on track at work. I began training my assistant, who turned out to be a fast learner and a hard worker. We were rocking right along until the next bump in the road. My husband became ill and could no longer care for our daughter. Picture this: I'm recovering from a traumatic event, I have a six-month-old baby, a sick husband and a business to run; easy peasy, right? To make a long story short, my in-laws took care of Audra during the day while I worked, then I took care of her at night until Kirk recovered. Once he was better, things got back on track in the office and at home. I took care of the business, while Kirk took care of things at home. My confidence and happiness were both at an all-time high. Sales grew, and the money was great. I worked long hours, but that's what a successful person does; they overcome. My first ten years with Company B were amazing. I met my goals and even exceeded my goals, winning trips to Cancun, Seattle, Orlando, Hawaii and more. However, I had no idea that change was on the way, and it was approaching fast.

My joy was interrupted when a huge bomb dropped; Company B went public. Soon the company's goals were centered on showing big profits for the investors. Agent contracts were drastically changed. We were all made independent contractors with ridiculous, unrealistic quotas. We lost our benefits and the capability of adding to 401Ks. Considering these major changes, Company B offered to buy us out at a low value. I allowed myself fifteen minutes of anger and then moved on. Little did I know that this shift was just the beginning of the end. Company B forced my fellow agents and I to sell products to clients that did not need them and even forced me to get a security license—suddenly, I was a financial planner, really? The pressure was horrible and ridiculous.

My book of business had always been profitable, but thanks to all the new rules, requirements and inflated rates, I lost long-term clients. That was when I realized I was stuck. Do you throw away 17 years? Or do you stay and allow yourself to be bullied and threatened by your "contract"? The pressure from work began to creep into other parts of my life. I had trouble sleeping, but who can sleep when they are not allowed to do what's best for their clients? Soon, anxiety crept in too and I landed in a major depression. It hit me hard and it broke my heart. The pain of losing my business, the one that I had built myself, felt like going through a divorce. I had let my carrier define who I was. Rather than allowing a myriad of aspects define my life and my business model, I had gotten hung up on building myself around a brand that no longer existed, at least in virtue. My mother taught me to always help people, but I was no longer able to help people.

I share this story of depression to help others. I advise you to never let your work define who you are. It's one of the worst things you can do. There will always be things you can't control. When I look back, I can see many of the business-related factors that contributed to my depression. I had all the classic signs: lack of sleep, lack of drive lack of confidence, and my frustration level was at an all-time high. I felt that I had built my business by myself and should not have to put up with the mess Company B had made of it. After missing an entire summer of work getting well, I sold my business. It was meant to be. In just a few months, I sold my book of business for my asking price. Once again, I found myself asking "now what?" All I knew was that I had to leave the pain of Company B in the past and I had to move forward.

The now-familiar search for a new company began for the third time. I looked around and weighed my best options. I took my time, spoke to many people and reviewed a variety of contenders. I ended up landing at "Company C." Unlike the parent corporations I had encountered in the past, this company was a true independent agency. The gentleman who founded Company C was himself a captive agent that got the raw end of the deal. He knows many agents face the same struggle I did. They become captive to a company that asks too much, gives too little and exchanges human decency for a glamorous profit margin. It was a place where I could retain my clients moving forward, but this time I had to start from scratch.

Unlike Company A, Company B was still in business. When I sold my Company B business, I agreed to a five-year Non-Compete Agreement, and I had zero intent to break that contract. So, I dove in and started again. It was not easy to say the least. I couldn't rely on big-name carriers to draw in new customers; however, I had a wide range of smaller carriers available. Diverse options such as those at my disposal allowed me to find policies that fit my clients' needs. I waved goodbye to lofty quotas and requirements to sell unnecessary coverage to unsuspecting customers. Company C has been well worth the investment of my time and money. I am equipped with exceptional resources and left alone to run my office and staff in whatever way works best for me. If I keep up compliance, no one interferes with my day-to-day operations. I am so happy to be a part of Company C.

Let's switch back to personal life for a moment. Kirk and I made it through our daughter's rebellious teen years and she went off to college. Life was going well, but here comes another thing. In early 2015, my mother was diagnosed with pancreatic cancer. I juggled work and traveling to Houston to visit my mom as much as I could. I could hardly believe this was happening. My mother was the strongest person I had ever known. My dad was heartbroken and dumbfounded by her diagnosis; he had no idea what to do or what steps to take. Don't get me wrong, my siblings helped too; however, my older brother's wife was also very ill. My sister-in-law died in the middle of September 2016. At her memorial, I realized just how sick my mother had become. I went back home and had the chance to refocus on work for about a week, before heading back to Houston. I had the honor of sitting at my mother's bedside for the last week of her life. As I sat with her, I finally realized how fast time goes. You hear that all your life, but you really don't pay much attention to it until the time starts to run out. Learn to allow time for your loved ones, no matter what. Never let your career take a higher priority than the people you're close to you. My mom passed away a mere two weeks after my sister-in-law. I had my laptop handy for the entire week I was with her, trying to keep up with work as much as I could. One huge responsibility that comes with owning your own company is finding a way to put the personal or emotional part of your brain on pause, so you can focus on business.

Now, it was time to plan a service for my mother. My brother had just lost his wife and my father was unable to process, so the task fell on me. I had never planned a funeral before. I hope my mom thinks I did a good job. Her service fell on a beautiful fall day, which is rare in Texas. It was bright and sunny outside with a soft, cool breeze in the air; I know she would have loved that day.

The loss was still fresh in my mind, but it was time to go back to work. Business was good, but as we rolled into 2017, I could feel God telling me to plan a trip with my family. When I look back, I am beyond grateful that I did. My siblings and I, along with their kids and some cousins, rented a beach house for a week that summer. During the trip, my brother mentioned a few weird symptoms he was having, but they didn't seem like anything serious. Well, here we go again. My oldest brother, the same brother that lost his wife and mother the year before, was diagnosed with cancer in August. He had glioblastoma; the most aggressive form of brain cancer. He tried surgery, chemotherapy and radiation, but nothing helped. Before his surgery, he asked me to take over as the executor of my father's estate, since he could no longer handle the matter. He also asked me to become the executor of his estate. So here I am, trying to process overwhelming grief, manage two estates, serve as power of attorney for two relatives, and run my business. My father is almost 93 years old; his decline in health at least makes sense. My brother's illness is something I don't think I'll ever understand. I've cried and pleaded with God over this, I can't even express the pain our entire family is feeling. As of this writing, he is still with us, but I know it won't be long. These are some of the major life events that have happened during my career. You must work through things, even when it seems impossible. I urge you to find a separation between career and family. Dedicate time and love to your family, but make time and headspace for your business, because the business will always go on. People aren't usually interested in hearing about your personal trials, but it can also be hard to talk about them, because people may perceive them as excuses. Unfortunately, you can't use life events as excuses. They won't allow you to take a "time-out" from your job. I'll say it again: life happens. It's not always fun and it's not always pretty, but the good news is that you can find ways to handle adversity. For me, separating my "work brain" and "home brain" works best. My personal life gets tumultuous, but my clients at work would never know.

The take away from my story is to never give up or give in. If you have a dream, keep chasing it. There will be many obstacles along the way, but each setback will build your character and provide you with an invaluable learning experience. I share my battle with depression as a story of hope. I don't doubt there are more stories like mine. Depression is a terrible illness; don't allow anyone or anything to trigger it. In my case, depression was situational, and I learned the hard way that I am not my career.

There will always be business and personal challenges. If running your own show were easy, everyone would do it.

CINDY BALSLEY

Cindy grew up in Houston with three siblings and parents that believed women were incapable of succeeding in business. She was supposed to grow up, get married and have babies – that was the life her parents had planned. Instead, Cindy decided to leave Houston and find her own way in the corporate world. After moving to Dallas in 1983, she worked under various insurance brokers and became an expert in the industry. Eventually, Cindy realized she was making great revenue for others and decided it was time to run her own show and make the big bucks herself. She was single and thought if she failed, at least she wouldn't be pulling an entire family down with her. With the support of close friends, Cindy set out on her own to build what would eventually become Balsley Insurance Group; a branch of The Woodlands Financial Group and Insurance Services. Years of experience have left Cindy well versed not only in the technicalities of insurance, but also in the important role of customer service. When she's not in the office with her husband Kirk, you can find Cindy volunteering at church or cuddling on the couch with her dog Mitch.

- https://cindybalsley.com/
- www.facebook.com/Balsley-Insurance-Group-114848921079/

ANGELA HOLT
One Day

"One day you will own a cafe where kids can play and have fresh, healthy food." What? Who? Me? That is what I would have said if someone told me years ago that this is what I would be doing in 2016. Even after two years in business, I am still amazed that I am the owner of Jungle Joe's and that it all came to fruition.

I've always loved kids and graduated with a Bachelor of Education from Southwest Texas State (now Texas State) University. However, after graduation, my path took me in a different direction. I had worked in restaurants during college, but little did I know (or if someone had told me I would have never believed them) that one day that experience would come in handy when I opened my cafe. After graduating, I moved to San Diego and got my real estate license and worked successfully for 15 years in both new home sales as the Marketing and Sales Manager and as a Real Estate Broker. After having our son, Chase, I decided that the cutthroat, 24/7-world of real estate was not my dream job! Therefore, after searching for over 2 years for my "what's next," I contemplated different scenarios! I had thought about going back to school or using my degree in education, but I had the entrepreneurial bug.

When my husband, Rick, retired from the Navy in 2015 we decided it was time to leave San Diego. We packed up our family (including my mom, dad, and grandfather) and headed for Frisco, Texas. I knew I wanted to open an indoor play business. After looking at the available spaces in Frisco and surrounding areas for a few months and losing out on what I thought was the "perfect" facility, we gave up. I got my real estate license in Texas, as did my husband. A week later, my husband drove by a space in Frisco that was much smaller than we had originally planned. A week after viewing the location, we signed the lease and worked with the city to obtain necessary permits and began demolition of the interior. No turning back! Little did I know the blessing of having the smaller space and that it would be one of the things our customers love about Jungle Joe's.

Two years later, business is great, and I love that kids have a safe place to play and parents have a cozy place to have a coffee and healthy meal and watch their kids have fun!

Even though I love what I do, I must admit there have been days that this road has been challenging, difficult and financially straining. My husband and I have financed every penny in opening Jungle Joe's and getting things up and running. I knew when we decided to be business owners that there would be trials and tribulations - and a lot of work. I was ready for the challenge. I soon found out that what I had read in books was true - "You don't know what you don't know until you know." You can plan, prepare spreadsheets with projections, create a business plan and start marketing the business, but until the open sign is on, the doors are unlocked, and you post on Facebook that you are open, no business owner knows what each day will bring. Even still, I don't.

Does this mean that if you are reading this you should not open your own business? No, not at all. We decided to take a huge leap of faith! And, when we veered from the path of opening Jungle Joe's, somehow, we kept getting pulled back in this direction. Everything I did in the past lead me to where I am today. I never thought I would leave California and live in Texas again. (I grew up in Round Rock, Texas.) But, here we are...in Frisco, Texas, one of the fastest growing cities in the United States and one of the wealthiest. This is good for business, but not always good for your psyche.

I am a big believer in all the material items that we possess are not important, and that if I have my family and friends, that is ALL that matters. Believing something and making it your reality are two different things. I'm a mom of a 10-year-old son who lives in an area where many kids are given what they want, when they want it. As parents, we want to give our children a great life and all the things they see other children have. Women are nurturers and hate to see our children upset about not getting that hoverboard he/she is begging for on their upcoming birthday. We live in a "Keeping Up with the Joneses'" world. This is our reality. Opening a business has given me a new perspective on how we raise our son. The juggling act of motherhood and business owner is tough. You work all day every day, then come home to dinner preparations, homework and bedtime routine. You are exhausted and would love to skip the 20-minutes of reading that evening. The financial burden of owning a business with overhead is constantly in your thoughts. It has helped us to see what is most important in our lives. Is it that hoverboard? No! Family time and memories, you share outweigh possessions. It's doing what you love and creating something that gives you satisfaction. This is a life lesson I think I needed.

The cutthroat world of real estate I mentioned is also hard work with many struggles, but there are a lot of financial benefits that came along with that hard work - minimal overhead, 30-40 day turn around for commission checks and the sky's the limit on earning potential. My family and friends still think I'm crazy for walking away from the money I was making. However, the future of Jungle Joe's, seeing it grow and what it has become gives me more satisfaction than anything I ever did in real estate. The risk is not for everyone! It is the most rewarding thing you can do if you are willing to work hard, and I mean really, hard, along with making sacrifices with your time, finances, and peace of mind.

The dream of Jungle Joe's (didn't know the name of the business at that time) all began one day in sunny southern California. Rick and I were sitting in an indoor play business near where we lived in North San Diego County. I was ready for a new career, but nothing seemed to be the right job for me. I knew that going back to school to teach was not the answer, but I wanted to work with kids. As we sat there watching our young son play, I quipped, "This place is always busy," and right then and there, I started running some numbers. It all seemed so easy. If you build it, they will come! It took over two years from that day until we were in Texas and looking for the location of Jungle Joe's. I visited every indoor play business around, even when we traveled. Our son became our Marketing Analyst, commenting on what he liked and did not like at each place we visited. I made mental notes of what I thought was a good idea and what I didn't want to do in my business. Even at this time of researching, I don't think I ever thought that our business would happen. I kept on talking about it to whoever would listen, and my sister-in-law started brainstorming names for the business and coming up with logos. While writing this chapter, I can't believe that initial conversation with Rick grew into our business in Frisco, Texas.

How glamorous it must be to own a business?!? You hire employees, you tell them what to do and they do it. You work behind the scene spending time with your family, volunteering at your son's school as the room parent for his class and help him with his homework. You cook great meals for your husband and travel with your family. Wrong! No one will ever know or care about your business as you do. Granted, I did (and still do) have a hard time passing the baton and delegating, but I'm working on it. Business ownership is hard. (I know I've already said that before.) I also know what you are thinking. How hard can it be? At least that is what I thought. I thought I was an organized, driven, motivated person that could do anything with the right resources. I knew it would be difficult, but I would work through the first few months of training everyone and things will run from there. The truth is, you will work 7-days a week! Business ownership is a job of many jobs - marketing, hiring and managing employees, business development, bookkeeping, and the list goes on and on. The enormity of it all can be overwhelming at times. Unless you have multiple partners, personal wealth or financial backing, the business owner must make sure every aspect of the business is completed. In addition, you worry about the expenses being paid and if customers will come through the door.

There were days when we first opened that I was so tired, that I couldn't keep my eyes open during the drive home after a 10-12-hour day. I was constantly on my feet and they hurt. It was not like in my 20's when I'd work a 12-hour shift at the Hula Hut in Austin, Texas, and hopped in the car to Don's Depot for a beer with friends and we would get up the next morning and do it all over again. But, I digress. My feet hurt like they have never hurt before. I needed those Epsom salt baths just to get my body moving again in the morning. I heard once that owning a business is buying yourself a job. This is so true. You do not have a boss, which was my number one criterion for a new career, but you will work harder and longer than you ever have in your life.

Stick with me here. The entire chapter won't be negative. I would be remiss if I didn't tell you my story of owning a business. Remember as you are reading, I love what I do. This is the path I was meant to take.

So how does one stay positive and make it work? "Success is never permanent, and failure is never final." This is my new motto. I have worked with the idea in mind of trial and error. There have been many errors, but we adapt, brush it off and keep moving forward. My husband is my biggest supporter. Although he does not run the day to day operations, he did allow me to take our life savings to start my dream business. This is a man who is not tolerant of risk, but he could see my passion for doing something different and went with it.

The joy of seeing the kids running through Jungle Joe's and the parents sitting and chatting with friends or working on their laptops is so rewarding. Having a customer ask "Are you the owner? This place is great. I love the food and that I can actually sit and relax." Another customer just recently told a staff member that our Cafe Latte was better than Starbuck. These kinds of comments make my day and only fuel my passion more. Even our struggles become a blessing. Two years into the business has given me a clearer picture of how our systems should be implemented and the departments must be formed. I am a better manager to the employees now. (I could write a book on working with the Millennials and Gen Z-ers. This, however, is for another time.) Our sales have grown substantially over the last year and the employee roles have changed. The day to day operations are manageable because I have a staff that knows what to do each day. Children's safety, cleanliness, and customer service are our top priorities.

My biggest motivation is Guy Raz *"How I Built This"* on NPR. My brother told me about this podcast and it has been a game changer. I listen to this on the days I have (make) time to go to the gym. Most of the business owners he has interviewed are creators of multi-million and, in some cases, even billion-dollar companies...and they didn't have an easy start. It took years and years for them to have a successful and profitable business. Some of them even failed at one and picked themselves up again to start another company. They were scrappy and started in their basements, working doing massages in their apartment or building things in their garages. They pulled all-nighters, working full time jobs and working on their business at night. You don't become big-time overnight. Sure, there are exceptions to this and we hear about them in the media, a lot...but growing big fast isn't always a dream come true either.

What are the first steps? Plan, plan, and then plan some more.

Your planning stages will be different depending on your business. I recommend reaching out to other business owners and community leaders in your area. Asking them what they would have done differently and first steps of getting things going. I would sit and have coffee with anyone that would talk to me.

Do as much research about the market you are thinking about entering. Go to competitors places of business and check out what they are doing. Now with the internet, finding information on competitors is not as time consuming as it once was. What makes you different? How will your business stand out? Why will customers come to see you or buy from you instead of the business down the road?

Networking. This was a curse word to me. Anytime someone would invite me to an event, I would politely decline. Speaking in front of a group, regardless of the size, was terrifying. I couldn't even get out a 30-second commercial without my heart pounding and fumbling over my words. Now I love it (or at least do not dread it like I once did). I have great relationships, including the women that have written other chapters in this book, from going to meetings and chatting with other professionals and hearing their stories. We all have a story! Do not be afraid to share your story with others. That is what makes you interesting and how you will be remembered...and it's your way of paying it forward. Your story could be the spark that ignites someone else's passion.

The local Chamber of Commerce is why we are still in business. That is right! I meant this statement and believe it wholeheartedly. Rick and I decided to go to our first networking event at the Frisco Chamber of Commerce shortly after Jungle Joe's opened. We were both so nervous. We were introduced to an Ambassador that told us how the meeting would go and that we could have 30-seconds to give a commercial. What? We had nothing prepared. We followed this poor lady around until the meeting started and I don't remember what I said when I stood up. I tell this story for those reading that also have this fear. That day changed our business. I have met with multiple professionals in many different fields I met through the Frisco Chamber. The Chamber employees are problem solvers. If you need help with something, they might get it done for you. I have been coached, trained and mentored by Chamber members. I have friends and happy hours with the Women Enhancing Business Group of the Chamber. If you are in a business and not a member of your local Chamber, you should check it out today.

When we first opened, we would advertise anywhere and everywhere - print advertising, send postcards through snail mail and, of course, online/social media marketing. I do not think that for the first year this was a bad strategy. We needed recognition. Slowly I realized I had cut back on marketing expenses. This morning at the gym I listened to NPR's "How I Built This" with Lululemon

Athletica founder, Chip Wilson. He said he only did break-even marketing. Ah-ha! That was what we were doing, and I did not know what it was called. I'm a people pleaser and when people would come into our doors at Jungle Joe's, I would want to buy what they were selling. This is not how a business owner should think! I started to cut down on all marketing expenses except local, community events. If the organizer of the event would allow us to come and set up a table to give away marketing pamphlets and do a raffle for a Safari Birthday Party Package at no cost or a small fee, we were there. We still go door to door to local businesses to hand out coupons. We cross market with other businesses in Frisco. You cannot stay in business if you are not active in social media and have an extensive online presence.

Business plans are not fun to write. Ugh. I hated this part. Since we did not require any financing, no one saw the plan except the insurance broker. You must write it all out. A business plan is just as much for you as it is for others that might need to see it. It will help you organize and give you a clear picture of your business. I still revisit my business plan. It's good to look back to see the plan and help remember our original strategy. Some things I thought we should do in the beginning were put to the side and can come back into play as we progress in the business.

Be strong - Reviews! They are essential for business. We have a lot of great review. For some crazy reason, I only focus on the bad ones. This is what keeps me up at night. I go over and over in my head how we could have made the experience better. This has been one of my biggest struggles, aside from employee retention. I've learned that we can comment on the feedback given by customers, which we do for every review regardless if it's good or bad and improve where improvement is needed.

Budgeting for both the business and home is our new reality. I spend many hours a week running numbers to see if our revenue meets the expenses. Our employee labor costs are always too high. How do I get food cost down? These and numerous other questions go through my head every day. It is hard for many people that have not been in business to know how much it costs to open their doors. When you add in the expenses of rent, employees, marketing, utilities, cafe food, and supplies, birthday party decorations and balloons, things add up quickly...quickly. I remember thinking when I was much younger and working in a restaurant, how could the cost of one cup being wasted or a meal being comped make a big difference. Believe me, when I tell you, it does. Every penny counts, especially when you first open a new business.

Forbes Magazine reports that 8 out of 10 businesses fail. According to the Small Business Association (SBA), "30% of new businesses fail during the first two years of being open, **50%** during the first five years and **66%** during the first 10." I know that even though I studied about owning a business and thought I knew what I was doing, I was not prepared. I have no formal schooling in business. I do not think I passed finance in college. Hitting the pavement running and learning from other people are more my style. We have only been in business for two years. These statistics are scary, but there are still 44% of businesses that make it through 10 years. This is how I look at it. Can we fail? Sure. I want to be in the 44%. If we fail, at least we tried, and I will use this experience to start another venture. "Let it go, let it go, can't hold it back anymore." We all know these are lyrics from the movie *Frozen*. They are in my head all the time. I must let things go and roll off my back. We all have negative thoughts running through our heads. (You probably already know what I'm talking about here!) The customer is always right, but sometimes they are also mean and infuriating. We strive for great customer service at Jungle Joe's. It is hard to hear as a business owner something you or your staff has done wrong -- but you must, you guessed it, let it go. Improve and move on.

My husband and I rely heavily on our faith. Regardless of your religion, faith is what can help on those days that aren't so great, it keeps you focused and grounded. I believe God has a plan and lead us from that day in California and the initial conversation at the indoor play business down this path. The "what next" conversation went from a scribbled-on napkin and formed into a growing business. I have done many things in the last two years I thought I would never do, including writing this chapter on "Being a Business Owner". Who am I to tell others how to start a business? Looking back on the last 3-4 years I realize what I have accomplished. My husband, friends, and family have been right by my side, through the thick and thin (and some tears), the entire way. Business ownership is not for everyone. My hope is for those that are on the fence or scared to take that first step, will take a leap of faith as well. They may be baby steps and plans will change as you progress, but you too will learn that although it is not easy, it can be the most rewarding things you can do. Knowing it will take hard work and some time, your dreams can also become a reality.

ANGELA HOLT

 Angela grew up just outside of Austin, Texas in a little town called Round Rock. Okay, it's not so little anymore, but being part of that small community was an important part of Angela's childhood. As 'small town' as this girl could have become, Angela has also traveled around the world. She lived in New Zealand and traveled extensively in Australia, Malaysia, Singapore & Europe, which gave her exposure to a multitude of perspectives and 'hometown' ideals.

Today, Angela's sense of community is something she relies on both professionally and personally. Relationships with neighbors and friends keep Angela busy. As a mother, working close to home and being active in the community are important aspects of Angela's life. She and her husband, Rick, have been married since 2005.

A licensed Real Estate Broker for over 15 years in San Diego County, Angela's real estate career began in new home sales. From there, she started working as a realtor for Coldwell Banker where she and her partner were always the leading sales team in the office, winning the highest award each year for sales volume. She then ventured out and started Kindred Real Estate in 2013.

When Rick retired from the US Navy in 2016, they took a leap of faith and moved to Frisco, Texas with the dream of opening an indoor playground and café for children. In 2016, Jungle Joe's opened and that dream became a reality! Angela's community spirit, professionalism, and commitment continue to drive her and have been passed on from her years in real estate to her customers at Jungle Joe's.

- https://www.facebook.com/junglejoesfrisco/
- https://www.instagram.com/jungle_joes/
- https://twitter.com/jungle_joes
- http://junglejoesfrisco.com/

LISA STUBBS
Recovering Perfectionist

Nicole Lynn (fearless, dynamic and amazing), Wave Maker organizer and leader, interviewed me and this is the general result ;)...

Introduction from Nicole: "It's been fun watching Lisa Stubbs grow as I met her over a year ago. Seeing the "behind the scenes Lisa" has been a joy and a privilege. She works with Monat, aka Modern Nature. When I met her, I loved watching her in her natural flow. She presented the products "informationally" and wasn't "sales pitchy," so I knew I could become her friend. Now I consider her very successful. She's a little more bashful about it, but she drives her free white Cadillac (free in that she doesn't pay for it; however, her hard work paid off), has gone on 4 earned trips from her company, which I think is fantastic. She also has a husband and 4 kids! Tell us a little bit about how Monat found you or how you started this journey as I'm sure you didn't wake up one day wanting to work for this type of company."

I'd like to set the stage, so you see how much Monat answered our prayers, impacted our family, and became part of the journey. Maybe you will relate to some of it.

After graduating from college in Youth Agency Administration, at age 24, I met and married my husband. I was working for a school district focused on "out-of-school time" children. I was overseeing summer and after-school programs as well as the Jobs For Kids program. My boss allowed me to bring my first daughter, Natalya (now 16), to work with me. I was 27. I remember carrying her around in my Baby Bjorn and hiring my sister and sister in law to come to babysit her when I had business meetings. The pay was hourly, so I worked 10-hour days as I squeezed in time to nurse her during the day as that was super important to me. Crazy, amazing blessing, right? Bring your child to work with you??!! It was very rewarding because of the impact it was making for low-income children (keeping them safe as latch-key children occasionally get into trouble because they are not supervised) and helping families whose parents both worked or single parents. I quit two months before my 2nd daughter, Jasmine (now 14), was born because I could not imagine wrangling a toddler and a baby working that job, that's when I became a stay at home mother.

To back up just a little, we experienced 2 miscarriages before the girls were born and then 3 more before the boys were born. We'd lose these babies typically at the end of the first trimester. Interesting side note...before the miscarriages, we were given paperwork on infertility as we had struggled with getting pregnant for over a year. The childbearing years were a roller coaster with so many tests taken to determine the cause of the multiple miscarriages. After each one, I felt very strongly about waiting 1 full year before attempting to get pregnant as I wanted to be emotionally and physically ready since there is a real grieving process involved with each one. It was a blessing to find out before our first son, Britton (now 9) was born, that I had an autoimmune issue which was the cause of the miscarriages (found through genetic testing). The main lesson learned: the Lord is in charge of the womb. He's in charge of everything ;). Our 4th child was born, Gunnar (now 7), at age 36, almost 37. One of the side effects of the autoimmune issue is that it negatively affects hair too and I was losing gobs of it in the shower.

Our savings account was drained when we moved to Texas because we found ourselves with two mortgage payments for 15 months. What a heavy burden! We had one good month after the home sold, so we took a vacation to Virginia Beach to visit his family and then the economy crashed. Since my husband is in advertising, that is the first budget cut companies make - lowering their ad dollar budget. He was still employed, it just wasn't enough for us to make ends meet for 7, yes, SEVEN years. We sold our other home and used money from the sale of that home every month to makes ends meet (thankfully we made quite a decent amount from the sale). We learned to be very frugal, washing plastic utensils, purchasing as many clothes as we could for our children from 2nd hand stores, holding garage sales, minimal date nights (that can make some stir crazy haha), etc. We did have some priorities, like allowing our girls to have one extracurricular activity so they would not feel the impact and stress we felt or feel like they were different from their friends (as we currently live in a very affluent area). I'll be honest, we tried not to look like we were struggling. We couldn't "keep up with the Jones'," but it felt like we were living a lie and that we didn't belong. Pretending that everything was okay while in public was exhausting. Honesty about our situation was given to close friends; however, I'm sure it was not fun for them to hear me complain, whine and let it out. I could feel them pull away. Besides, who wants to be around a "Negative Nellie" or an Eeyore from Winnie the Pooh?!

Social media played a part too as I got caught up in "comparison-itis," comparing myself with other people. Watching others take so many vacations, remodel their home, buy nice things, etc. My thought process was not as healthy as I was believing Satan's lies that we didn't deserve anything but stress and misery. One of my greatest struggles was that I was losing my confidence and self-esteem though...I even felt the way I looked was drastically changing. My hair being dry, damaged, limp and stringy did not help me feel confident. I still remember cringing when someone would sit behind me because they'd be able to see my split ends visibly.

Can anyone relate to that?! Why do we sometimes care so much about what other people think of us?

I turned inward, becoming very introverted. When I was at home, it was like I was in hiding. If someone came to the door, I would tell the kids to be quiet and wait for them to leave, even if I knew who was on my front porch. I would avoid answering the phone, even if I knew it was one of my in-laws! I needed to know what people wanted ahead of time, so I could be prepared. I didn't get out of the house much as a stay at home mom, so there was not too much adult interaction, which impacts people. Don't get me wrong, I could "pretend" and put on a happy face when we were at church or school functions. Like the "Sunday Morning" YouTube video!! If you haven't seen it, you'll get a kick out of it. The moral here is that Nobody is perfect, not even the family sitting in front of you. Looking back, I realize I was battling anxiety (we exhaust ourselves because we tell ourselves one thing when the reality is usually something different), and possibly some minor situational depression. Stress also impacts our hair.

I've learned a lot over the past 3.5 years. At the time I was going through these issues, I didn't know about some of the science behind hair. For example, I have learned that our hair shows the results of what's happening internally. Very interesting to note is the fact that 2-3 months after you've had a fever, surgery, stress etc., that is when it manifests itself in your hair. For those that are affected by hair loss, you need to think back to what was going on 2-3 months ago to find clues as to why you are experiencing hair loss issues. The average person loses up to 50-100 hair strands per day, that's normal. Our hair goes through phases, so hair shedding is a natural phase of life (some notice it more than others).

Back to my experience, I was losing gobs of hair in the shower, which was nerve racking! This was not the normal 50-100 strands per day! I was not ready at this age to have people be able to see my scalp through my hair. I felt too young! I was 37! How was that happening to me?! This impacted my self-confidence, after all, they say hair is 50% of our look, right?! Being a stay at home mother after being in the business world for almost 10 years was a difficult transition too. I found myself being the kind of mother who wanted my kids on a schedule to get their naps eat, and then play. This allowed me to stay ahead of some of their meltdowns; however, it impacted a social schedule for myself (there wasn't much of one). I know there are many wonderful ways to mother and I don't feel one is necessarily better than another. We need to find a way that works for us. Thankfully, I had a friend, Heather, refer me to Fly Lady, and I found changing my perception of things helped drastically. Instead of doing the laundry, I was blessing the clothes. Instead of cleaning the family room and picking up toys, I was doing a "5-minute room rescue". Self-care was not a priority either, so I recommend moms taking time for themselves! Fill your own cup ☺.

Through the years, my hair stylists would reassure me that my hair would go back to normal once I was done having kids. When that chapter was over, and my hair issues/concerns were still there, I was desperate for help! I'd been trying the top of the line shampoos (they'd plateau after a couple of months), sulfate free shampoos (hair never looked good), and Nioxin (did not eliminate the hair thinning). I went to an internal medicine doctor who ran all kinds of labs on my blood, everything came back normal, so she recommended I use biotin. I used it for 6 months, and she had me switch to a different brand because there was no change. The same thing happened again with the 2nd brand. At that point, I turned to Eastern medicine. I sought out a holistic chiropractor (for 1.5 years) that had me use many supplements. I'm sure they helped my body in some way; however, they did not change the status of my hair. I started to learn more about toxins. Did you know? It only takes 26 seconds for toxins to enter our bloodstream once they touch our skin because that's the most porous membrane we have. One can see here that another priority was my hair with our budget. Even my husband knew it was necessary for me to be on this journey to find relief.

A friend of mine, Breila, introduced me to Monat. She knew I was struggling with major hair frustrations. She'd been introduced to Monat by a friend of a friend. Breila is into living a toxin-free lifestyle too. She ended up being completely impressed with the ingredients the products did NOT contain yet didn't think the products would perform because most sulfate free shampoos simply don't. Yes, your hair/scalp is healthier, but your hair doesn't look super beautiful. After she asked her mother to be a guinea pig (who has androgenetic alopecia), she asked me if she could add me to a Facebook Group - MONAT Hair Care - Personal Stories. At 11pm when I climbed into bed, I could not stop reading testimonials. I wanted my hair to look like those After pictures (their hair looked so healthy, shiny and beautiful!!)! I went to see her a few days later, and she used the products in my hair. I went home and could not keep my hands out of my hair. It was so soft and smooth feeling. I researched the company since it was only 2 months old as I wanted to be sure it wasn't being made in someone's garage (I had NEVER researched a product before purchasing it before). I loved the fact that I could get my money back if I was not happy. I was never offered that by the doctors' offices, the holistic chiropractor or the other shampoo brands that I had used. It didn't feel like it was a risk (we were not risk takers back then haha). I'd found a video about the founding family, the Urdanetas, and was drawn into their goodness and hearts. They talked about how they are dedicated to family, service, and gratitude. I admired that as those things resonated with me due to my upbringing (I love my parents!). I felt compelled to give them my business because they inspired me. I could feel they were genuine. They drew me in. I bought a product pack, with absolutely NO intention of owning my own business. I just wanted the deepest discount, and I did not have to make monthly purchases or meet sales quotas, phew! Besides, there are 6 people in my family, that's a lot of heads to test the products on!

After 3 weeks of using the products, my hair stopped falling out in handfuls in the shower. After 3 months, people asked me what I had done to my hair?! I didn't share how to get the products for 5 months of using it, however so many wanted to know what my secret was. It was a no-brainer by that point. I never dreamed changing my shampoo would change my life; however, it truly has! Not only did it transform my hair, it also restored my confidence, and now I feel like I've come back to life. If I didn't feel like getting up some mornings, I knew my team needed me. Helping others start their businesses and assisting others with their hair goals or scalp concerns has healed my heart. I truly believe this company is a personal development company disguised as a network marketing company. It's social selling and most shop online. Meeting so many people has forever blessed my life because I've learned so many tips and seen so many beautiful traits in others that I work on emulating. I love who I am now! I have so much purpose. The businessman in my husband realized quickly that this could be a huge opportunity and he is ever so supportive! He allowed me to work hard to achieve Monat's USA Founder status (which means if you reached a certain level in the compensation plan within the first year of signing up - within the company's first year in business - you could claim that status). I have felt humbled by being led to this opportunity (prayers of gratitude inserted here ;).

I won't tell you my whole life story; however, we get told a lot of things growing up (whether we believe them or not is what's important) that shape us. We experience things, good and bad. These things mold us. I grew up in San Jose, and then before 5th grade, we moved to Pleasanton, CA. I remember my shirt tags being pulled and they would read what the labels were and told others. I learned quick what the good brands were. Before this, I didn't even know there was a difference in brands or that it even mattered. I informed my mother that I could only wear Guess, Espirit, and wished I could wear Benetton (but that one was out of the question). My mother took us to the San Francisco clothing outlets, so I could find some that were less expensive. There was another set of girls that referred to themselves as "The Group." If I remember correctly, there were 9 girls involved. My friend and I wanted to join it. My friend could buy them glitter and nail polish. I had nothing to give. They voted over our acceptance during lunch. My friend made it in, and I did not (due to 5 votes against me joining). These girls were the "popular" girls that would listen to Madonna on their Walkman's outside of our classrooms. My how that made me feel "less than." I have been interested in fashion, ever since. I may not have always looked like it though, especially during child-birthing years ;).

The better YOU feel you look, the better YOU feel inside. In college, I took a course called, Aesthetics of Dress. The instructor taught us that if you can only afford one nice outfit that compliments your body and you feel amazing in it, wear it EVERY day! Don't get me wrong, beauty does come from WITHIN; however, people typically need a clean, well-groomed appearance to boost their self-confidence. If you dress like a slob, you'll feel like a slob. If you dress for a job interview, you feel more inclined to act professionally. Enhancing our beauty is important, even though beauty comes from WITHIN! I've heard it said, our eyes are the window to our soul. As we take in personal development to become the best version of ourselves (which I consider "light"/goodness), the more "light" we can emanate and share that light, uplifting/serving others. We must fill our cups with self-care, so we have the energy to give. It's just like the oxygen masks on the airplane. We must first put ours on first, so we can be alive to assist those who need help putting their masks on. Confession: one of the first things I did after having some success with Monat was to hire a clothing stylist/fashion designer, Vanessa, to clean out our master closet and take me shopping to overhaul my wardrobe. Who knew having 14 cardigan sweaters in different colors was a fashion faux pa! Truly, it was just not the look for me with my new business and all, even though there is nothing wrong with having a few sweaters.

During college, I spent some time with psychologists, counselors, and even a psychotherapist as my minor was in Family Science and getting deeper into my psyche was very intriguing to me. One of my counselors would not work with us unless we took on the assignments given. He challenged me not to wear make up for 2 weeks! I compromised and said the Lord wants us to look our best on Sunday, I need to wear makeup on the 2 Sundays. He agreed. My lesson learned here was that no one, not one person said a word about not having any makeup on. No one asked me why I wasn't wearing any. I had been telling myself I could only go out in public with my make up on because I cared too much about what others thought about me.

Along with this entrepreneurial journey in the beauty industry, I've learned a lot about myself, and I've grown a lot. My life experiences have made me realize that I'll be successful in business if I can help people with their looks, hopes, and dreams. It's not all about the sale. That's what amazes me the most. It's about having great relationships with others. It's about being kind. It's about listening to other people's needs. It's about helping others and lifting others up. If a sale happens naturally, then fantastic! Surrounding myself with people who are doing the same thing has been such a blessing. Who knew one could have so many friends?! This is the biggest treasure of all!! Learning to focus on having a servant's heart is key.

I tried so hard to "fit in" and make people happy so I would have their approval. What I've learned is this, business life is a journey, and you won't reach the goals you want by faking it (maybe some can lol) and you won't get there overnight. Don't get me wrong, in the beginning we may need to fake it until we make it! I allowed a lot of my experience to shape me into a perfectionist. I second guess so many decisions I make. I'm afraid I will make the wrong one and regret it. This might not sound like a big deal, however if you are a perfectionist, you know what I'm talking about. You hold yourself to a higher standard. You are way too hard on yourself. The voice in your head tells you that you are never good enough. We have between 50,000-70,000 thoughts EACH day! It's A LOT to manage, especially when they are in a negative cycle. According to Michelle Manske, "Perfectionism, when taken to its extreme, has negative consequences. It can lead to workaholism, eating disorders, over-training, social anxiety, body dysmorphia, chronic stress, obsessive-compulsive disorder, depression, insomnia, and heart disease." Think about it, how many Hollywood celebrities suffer from this? I know I was impacted by social anxiety, situational depression, mild insomnia, over-training (at the gym and with work because I wanted to prove something) and workaholism for about 2.5 years in this business (until Nicole Lynn came around and taught me about Time Blocking #gamechanger).

She teaches that "Perfectionism is the quest for unrealistic standards. It's characterized by a compulsive striving for perfection, equating self-worth to achievement, being highly self-critical and judgmental, persistent dissatisfaction, paralyzing fear of failure, and a tendency to procrastinate until things are 'just right.'" Perfectionism can be paralyzing! I know I've lost loads of business because I've been too afraid to follow up with someone, just felt too nervous. It's like self-sabotage. Self-destruction. Even fear of reaching one's potential.

Want to know how to avoid it? I'll tell you :). Learn to recognize it and where it stems from. Change your "fear of failure" thought process to "I can do this." Accept yourself with love. Know that most people are not paying any attention to you or what you're doing all the time. Be careful with procrastination. This is a success killer! Allow yourself to make mistakes. Abraham Lincoln and Winston Churchill said, "Success, it has been said, isn't the absence of failure, but going from failure to failure without any loss of enthusiasm." If any of these items are the biggest issue for you, I'd advise you to do research and find out what you can do to overcome it. I am still in a battle with some of these things because they don't instantly go away once you identify them. It takes time to change a lot, and I must remind myself sometimes that 'I am His daughter and I am worth it.' "Success is on the other side of fear." "I am grateful for my challenges because they help me find my courage" (authors unknown).

Another way I have found MASSIVE assistance is from a skill I learned about. A year ago, I earned a leadership training in Dallas. It was put on by the people behind Success Magazine. One of the speakers was Mel Robbins, from CNN. She has a YouTube video called, "How Mel Robbins Curbs Her Anxiety in 5 Seconds." She talks about how NASA's space shuttle had a countdown before take-off. She watched it, and the next morning she used the 5 Second Rule, and she got out of bed right away, instead of lying there thinking about how she didn't want to get up or how she was still tired, etc. This rule has even helped some people not to commit suicide. She had a guest there whose life it saved! We need to teach this easy, free skill to our children and those we talk to. We never know the impact it could have on someone.

I hope and pray I am approachable. I guarantee you I do not bring judgment to the table. One of my rules is to look people in the eye (instead of up and down) because that is who they are, their soul is on the inside. First and foremost, give YOURSELF some grace/love.

Closing Tips:

Allow yourself to DREAM!! BELIEVE you can ACHIEVE!! Come up with a very strong "Why." We must get to the root of why we want a certain outcome. Create a business plan with goals in writing (there's something about putting pen to paper!!). This helps us with the daily decision to act toward our goals. It will help us start to feel intrinsically motivated. By breaking big goals into small steps, we can make big things happen. Being consistent over time will create momentum. If you're in network marketing, read or listen to *GoPro* by Eric Worre. Look at your morning mindset. Reclaim it if you're giving it away to others. Look at the book Morning Miracle if you need ideas. These things are simple, not easy. That's probably why not everyone is doing it because it seems like it should be harder (just like the leper being asked to wash himself 7 times to be healed in the Bible). Be sure to have a Gratitude Journal to record at least 1-3 things each day that you're grateful for. It takes about 1 minute, and it's proven this is an emotional healer. "What we focus on, we get more of." -Dr. Becky Bailey

Know that confidence and happiness are an ongoing choice. Choose mentors to listen to and get a book recommendation from them. After you read it, get another, etc. Life is not perfect (He never said it would be easy, He only said it would be worth it), kids are not perfect (mine are J/K), marriages are not perfect (we've been through some things and realized if we don't work together, those things will drive us apart), and business is not perfect (it always has ups and downs). I'm sure you can all relate. We all go through trials to help us get stronger and be able to know the good from the bad. Life is what we make of it, so take risks and make YOUR dream life happen! We can't go wrong with being ourselves and speak from the heart. Take time for self-care, filling our cup. We must start by getting in control of a few thoughts if we want to start making a change. And to reduce stress/adjust your mindset, take a listen to the TED Talk by Kelly McGonigal, "How to make stress your friend." This is revolutionary info here and it's only 15 minutes. Trust me, it's worth it for your thoughts and make sure you pass it on to help someone else.

LISA STUBBS

Lisa J Stubbs, first and foremost is a daughter of God, wife to Sterling of 19 years heading toward eternity, and mother of four fun children, and resides in Frisco, Texas. She grew up in the San Francisco Bay Area and loves being Texan. Her lifelong passion has been to help others, especially women feel beautiful inside and out. Lisa's love for others started at a young age by volunteering at religious youth camps and has continued into her career working with educational programs for nearly a decade. Lisa graduated in Youth Agency Administration under Recreation Management. She used this degree for 9.5 years overseeing summer and after school programs for a school district. She was also the Jobs For Kids Coordinator and was a National After School Accreditation Endorser and served on the National School Age Care Alliance. Lisa took a break from the educational system before her second daughter was born to focus full time on raising children. Now she has found a new passion as a hair consultant with Monat Global, a botanically based Anti-Aging Hair Care company and has quickly risen as a Mentor and USA Founder for Monat, while Monat has become the #1 premium hair care brand in America! She enjoys spending time with her family and friends, volunteering weekly as an aide for a darling 6-year-old Autistic boy, vacationing, exercising, working on living a healthier lifestyle, eliminating toxins from the home, reading, self-improvement, and making hair great again...one head at a time ;).

- Cell Phone (call or text): 469-712-7023
- Website: SweetHair.MyMonat.com
- Email: SweetHair92@gmail.com
- Hair Quiz: HairQuiz.MonatGlobal.com/SweetHair
- Facebook: SweetHair or Lisa J Anderson Stubbs
- Instagram: lisajstubbs92 or Lisa J Stubbs SweetHair

LISA STATZER
The Journey

"What do you want to be when you grow up?" I remember getting asked that question as a child. Back then I wanted to be a singer on the stage. I used to beg my friends to have talent contests so I could sing and win. No takers.

In contemplating that question, I always dreamed that my life's work would have a singular purpose. You find a career you love so much that it doesn't seem like work at all, but my career took me on a much different path.

It only took one year of teaching middle school to squash that dream. I accepted a position in a low-income school where neither the teachers nor students wanted to be there. I decided that there was something better for me, so I left the teaching field to find it.

I spent time in corporate America as a technical recruiter, but my heart was somewhere else. I remember driving home and thinking there must be something more.

My husband and I thought it would be a fun idea to start a business and family at the same time! Talk about stress and crazy ups and downs. I'm grateful for that decision because we've learned better communication and have grown closer together because of it. My husband continues to run that business today.

I've had my fair share of experience starting my own businesses and ending them. I have left a trail of direct marketing businesses in my past and even a nonprofit. Over the years, I dropped the belief that there would be one grand purpose in my life's work, and I've found excitement in pursuing different passions.

Now I find myself in a career of health and life coaching that is challenging, rewarding, and something I love. I wake up every day energized and curious about where the day will lead me. I imagine who I will have the honor of encouraging and inspiring today.

It all started when my dad was diagnosed with type 2 diabetes. In helping him, I realized that so many others needed the same guidance to lower their blood sugar naturally so that's how my business, Pre-Diabetic Support was born.

I have assisted loved ones in improving their health and lengthening their lives. I have encouraged students to push beyond physical limitations and accomplish goals they didn't think their older body could do anymore. This is a role that allows me to use my strengths of connecting with people, educating people, and being their cheerleader.

It has taken a lot of pushing myself out of my comfort zone to get where I am today. It's also taken a lot of soul searching and tears. The most amazing thing about my journey isn't just where I find myself today but the many lessons I've learned along the way.

It's these lessons that made life coaching a natural transition for me. I have a desire to help others make their life the best it can be. Isn't that what we all want?

Lesson #1: An end to a business does not mean failure

Often when a job ends, it's because you're going on to bigger and better opportunities. When a business ends, that's rarely the case. I've invested my money, my time and my dreams into many business opportunities that haven't been successful.

I'll admit that it's never easy to look at a business ending and see it as anything except a failure. Calling it a growth opportunity sounds like a phrase people use just to make you feel better about it. But the truth is, if you can embrace it as a growth opportunity, you will be so much stronger and more prepared for the next business opportunity.

Because we know there will be another one, right? I'm talking to all the serial entrepreneurs out there. You'll try again. Why? Because entrepreneurs all yearn to build something. To build something we can look at and say, "I did that!" We all yearn to serve our customers and community. The desire to own a business and work your best at it doesn't stop just because your business didn't make it. I think the desire grows and then it's not an "if" but "when" you will start the next one.

With each of these opportunities, I've improved my business skills in sales, marketing, and leadership. I've cultivated relationships that still impact my life today. Most importantly, I've more learned about myself. I've learned about my fears, how I doubt myself and what really motivates me. I've learned that it's in my heart and soul to build a business that serves others and allows my family to live a life of flexibility and independence.

All my past businesses have prepared me to serve my clients in my role as a health and life coach with much more skill, confidence and grace than I would have without those past challenges.

Lesson #2: Don't wrap up your identity in your job or business.

I love to attend networking meetings. There's a room full of people who want to grow their business through relationship marketing. When I meet someone new, I get excited to find out what they do and how I can help them. The synapses in my brain started firing and figuring out who I can connect that person with to help their business. I love learning about connections I have with people I've never met before. "Oh, you know so and so, too!" "Your kid plays lacrosse, too?" Cue the "We're all in this together " music. In that one room, you can see we all have something in common. That we're all connected in this world for a common purpose. You might think that purpose is something different than I do but it's inevitable that we're all in this creation of life together.

Even though I believe all of that to be the case, we're ultimately there to grow our business and make more money. Hence the most popular opening question, what do you do? We all know this question so well and answer it without any hesitation or giving it much thought. But I've been networking in my hometown for ten years on behalf of many different business ventures: two different multi-level marketing businesses, our foundation repair business that my husband runs, my nonprofit that I started and closed two years later, and a local women's league that I have been a member for thirteen years.

For someone whose goal was to find the profession that would fulfill me for the rest of my life, networking for a new business venture felt a little like I was changing not just my profession but also my identity. Like I was asking myself, "Who am I?"

I mixed up who I WAS with what I was DOING at the time.

There is more to a person than the work they do. I have learned to embrace my whole being. I identify with my love for life, my values, my faith, my relationships and my work. When we associate ourselves with all parts of who we are then when one part of our life changes or goes in a wrong direction, the core of who we are is still there. That gives us the resiliency to succeed even in the face of change.

Lesson # 3: Don't be afraid of change. Embrace it.

I have this overwhelming desire to organize my life so that it's manageable, fulfilling, joyful and stays that way forever. Surely you see the humor in this. I believe that God does, too. I love the Yiddish saying , "Man Plans, and God Laughs." Not that I believe he's laughing at us in a mean way but that he's amused at our inability to see how little control we have over outside forces that affect our lives.

Change is a constant. I have learned that my life is much easier when I embrace it. I'm still working on it, but I have made leaps and bounds since I made the difficult decision to close my nonprofit.

I started Give Back Collin County as a resource for nonprofits. For two years I ran it with an amazing team of ladies who I hand-picked because of their dedication to bettering our community.

After a yearly planning session, I felt very unsettled. I'd felt that way before the meeting, but I pushed it back. I thought having a clear direction for our nonprofit would take care of the feeling that I wasn't going in the right direction

When I was honest with myself, I needed a change. I was proud of myself because after coming to that realization, I acted quickly. How many times do we look at an uncomfortable situation and are paralyzed by fear to make a clear decision and then act on it? I know I had done that in the past.

Making the decision to close my nonprofit has been a hard one but it empowered me to seek other changes in my life. I chose "CHANGE" as the word that I would focus on for the rest of the year. You may remember that I said that I was the person who wanted to perfect her life and have it remain like that. Embracing and even seeking out change put me on a path of growth and opportunities that I never expected.

I changed things like my morning routine. I read more personal development books and challenged myself to think differently. I experimented with juice cleanses and different diets to see how I would feel. I meditated, read my bible more and really connected with God on a higher level than ever. The biggest change I made was how I dealt with stress and the effects that it had on my body. I even got a tattoo of a butterfly to commemorate all the changes I had been making.

With my work to embrace change, I still find myself sometimes desiring the comfort of predictability. When I do, I remind myself that change equals growth. Without growth our lives would be predictably, perfectly boring! And who wants that?

Lesson #4: Be Kind to Yourself

I am a very forgiving person for the wrongs that people inflict on me and others. I give grace freely when people make mistakes. I can say this confidently because my friends have told me this through the years.

Who do you think I'm the least forgiving of and give the least amount of grace to? You guessed it: me. It shows up in negative self-talk when I doubt myself when tasks get hard or berate myself when I mess up.

This all came to a head when I was running my nonprofit. I was having a bad day and confessing all my doubts about my abilities to my best friend. I was being much more vulnerable than usual. I took off the "everything is okay" mask which we wear most of our lives. She was amazed at how hard I was being on myself since I'm not like that with other people. She was also feeling a lot of insecurities around her work and juggling everything in life. A good girl talk did us both a world of good.

Around that same time, I had a therapist point out the same thing to me. I was kind to everyone except myself. Being kinder to myself means focusing on my thoughts. When I start to go down that path, I stop and ask myself, would I judge someone else this harshly?

I'm trying to teach this to my daughters, too. When they say negative things about themselves, I stop them, and we talk about it. I talk to them about not comparing themselves to others and being kind and patient with themselves. I ask them if this negative comment they are making about themselves even true. Usually, it isn't.

My youngest was complaining about her stomach being big. You would laugh at the thought because she is so tall and thin. But instead of dismissing her feelings, we talked about them. We talked about being kind in talking to ourselves. We also talked about the reality of her physique which is super skinny, but I tried not to focus on that. God made us all different and beautiful was the lesson.

I left my daughter's room feeling very successful as a mom and waking a bit taller. I walked into my bathroom and caught a glimpse of myself in the mirror. I had no makeup on and my hair was in a messy ponytail. I said out loud to myself, "Boy, I look like crap!"

I stopped in my tracks and laughed to myself. Did I just say that after discussing being kind to ourselves with my daughter? I'm still working on being kind to myself also and remembering that my words matter.

As a parent, you can be a positive role model by showing appreciation for your body by talking positively about yourself around your children. Well, all the time would be great but especially around your children.

Being kind to ourselves means not judging ourselves so harshly. Judging people, especially ourselves, is such a common practice that we don't even realize it when we do it. Pay attention to the thoughts that come to your mind when you think of how well you are performing that day, what you look like, or any other thoughts you have about yourself. Ask yourself am I being kind? What would I say to anyone else in this situation? Let's be our own biggest cheerleader!

Lesson # 5: You have the power to change your life and it starts with your thoughts.

The two biggest areas that my new approach impacted were my internal thoughts and my spiritual life. My internal thoughts at the time were filled with doubt and fear. Do you ever feel captive to thoughts that are swirling around in your head? Your thinking is foggy and it's hard to concentrate because you are constantly thinking about failure instead of accomplishing what you want.

The negative thoughts can be very powerful but not as powerful as you are. The problem is that even though we know the negative thoughts are not good for us, we often feel very comfortable in them. You may have gotten caught in this trap. It's easier to sit there and feel bad for ourselves and lament over how awful our life is instead of taking the energy and self-discipline it takes to find our way out of the darkness.

Our mind will believe negative thoughts easier than positive thoughts. So, we must work hard to bring in the light and positivity. I believe God gave us a great tool for this. Gratitude. The bible preaches it. Buddha talked about it. All major religions consider gratitude as being a way to worship and rise above our circumstances. I say rise above our circumstances because we are to be grateful for everything we have and everything that happens to us. That's a big order!

Gratitude plays a big role in turning our negative thoughts around, especially when we look for things to be grateful for when we aren't happy with how our life is going. Magical things happen when you practice gratitude. Practicing gratitude isn't just saying that you're thankful for something. It's feeling thankful.

Try it. Sit, close your eyes, and think of someone that you are thankful for. Think of how they make you feel. How eternally grateful that you are that they are in your life. Feel it in every cell in your body and sit in it for a however long you want. Think I'm crazy? Do it and you will immediately feel a heaviness lifting. Do it every day, even every hour, and you can change your life. Because your thoughts become your words and your words become your actions.

Changing your thoughts is the essence of changing your life. Gratitude is a great place to start when you need help changing negative thoughts.

During my year of changes and since then, I've kept gratitude journals and meditated on things I'm grateful for. When people bug me, I think of reasons I'm thankful for them. Sometimes it's easy and sometimes it's not, but it's always rewarding.

The most amazing result from this is my closer relationship with God. It started with being grateful for EVERYTHING. I voice being grateful for hot water, healthy food, the birds singing, my dogs, electricity, and my favorite shirt that keeps me warm. When you list five things a day and try not to have much repetition, you start opening your eyes to the beauty in your life.

It hasn't stopped there. It's allowed me to create a connection with God so I can now hand over my worries to him, my doubts, fears, and frustrations. It's a daily practice and I still sometimes choose to sit in my negative thoughts. Then I decide that's enough and release it all to Him.

Focusing on changing your thoughts will have a profound transformation in your life. If you make it a daily practice and let your thoughts become your words and your words become your actions, you can live a life of joy.

Lesson #6: Stress doesn't have to be constant.

I was lying on the table of a Chinese Medicine doctor when I had one of the biggest epiphanies of my life. It's funny how one simple question can bring amazing clarity. How one thought can change everything. I told you thoughts were powerful!

You see, I never learned how to deal with stress in my life. When things got tough and stressful, I only knew to put my head down and power through. That way of thinking benefited me in the short term during some very difficult and stressful times. It got me through college, my first year of teaching, and my daughter's toddler years.

In the long term, it crippled my neck and shoulders with muscle tension and pain for years. I went to doctors and chiropractors to alleviate the pain, but all their treatments only gave temporary relief. I had mostly given up on working out and spent my evenings rolling my neck and shoulders with foam rollers and lacrosse balls to get relief.

As I laid on the Chinese Medicine doctor's table, she mentioned that the top of my shoulders where my pain was concentrated was the decision-making part of the body. The she asked, "do you have any big decisions that you are trying to make?" I did. That was the precise time that I was deciding what to do with this nagging feeling that I needed to leave my nonprofit.

If I were in a cartoon at the time, you would have seen the light bulb go off above my head. The pain that I was experiencing wasn't just caused by a physical problem but a psychological one. Scenes from my life flashed through my mind of stressful times and how much of a toll the stress took on my emotions and physical body.

Shortly after, I found a doctor who I will be eternally grateful to who explained that, instead of dealing with my stress in a positive way, I tensed up my shoulders. After years of doing that, it created so much tension that most doctors were not aggressive enough in their treatment to break through it.

Well, let's just say that Dr. Wu was aggressive enough. It took months of painful treatments, but he released me from the pain. My muscles were so tight in the beginning that I broke an acupuncture needle!

Stress may manifest itself differently for you. You may have headaches or a different pain. It may make you impatient and easily frustrated with those that you love, thus hindering your relationships. It's endless the negative ways that stress can impact you.

There is a way out and it starts where so many positive changes in our lives start, our thoughts. How do you change those stressful thoughts when they are swirling in your head, clawing for attention, and dominating your mind? Meditation.

Meditation has moved out of the shadows of being something New Age and weird to mainstream due to its many benefits. I meditated every day for months to help calm my mind and I still practice it. The benefit is the ability to stop your negative thoughts, clear your mind, and choose empowering thoughts. Meditation is so powerful because it gives you a way to practice daily what is hard to do in the beginning of conquering stress and anxiety. Choose your thoughts.

There are many other things that I do to keep my stress levels down like making sure that I take time for family and friends and, most importantly, take time for myself. Having clarity about what's important in your life helps you focus on your priorities which can bring down your stress level, too. But of all of those and many more, meditation is by far the tool that helps me the most.

Situations still arise that give me stress. I will feel a tension in my shoulders and my neck will become tight. At that time, I realize that I have a choice. I can choose to stop, breathe deeply, and choose my thoughts or spiral down into anxiety, pain, and ultimately regret for letting myself go there. You will find that, with practice, the choice is easier to make and carry out.

Lesson #7: Find Your Tribe for Support

My family is incredibly supportive, especially my husband. We have been building businesses together for many years and even though we don't always agree, we always have each other's back. Having that support is vital.

Having that support in a friend group or tribe takes you to a different level. I am blessed to have a tribe of women who support me, love me and are also on an entrepreneurial journey. There are four of us and we all own our own businesses. We hang out socially, but we also meet so often just to talk about our business. We take turns discussing our goals and where we need help. We ask each other the hard questions and give honest feedback with grace and love.

Friendships become harder to find and maintain when you become adults. Our lives get so busy with work and spending time with your spouse and children. It's hard to find time to keep up with friends.

Be intentional with your time. Spend time with people who are positive. Find a group of people who are on the same journey as you use your collective experiences and wisdom to propel you all forward. You can do this in your professional life and your personal life. Mom's groups are a great example of this.

The ladies in this book, the Wave Makers, are another great example of utilizing a group for support. We support, teach, and cheer each other on to meet our weekly business goals. If you still can't think of an existing group that would work for you, start your own! You can make your life more meaningful and contribute to others who need your support.

I'm at a point in my life where my experiences and the lessons that I've learned have given me the desire to help others discover their best life. One of our inalienable rights is the right to pursue happiness. As a health and life coach, I can give my clients the strategies and tools to pursue a meaningful, fulfilling life where they are reaching their full potential and creating their own amazing experiences.

LISA STATZER

Entrepreneur

Lisa is a born and raised Texan who considers herself honored to serve others as a health and life coach. She and her husband are entrepreneurs at heart and can't imagine doing anything but running their own businesses. She has been married for over 20 years and has two wonderful daughters.

She enjoys being active in her community and volunteering. As a member of Frisco Women's League for 13 years, she has held various leadership roles. She served on their board of directors for 5 years as Vice President of Special Events, President, and Board Advisor. She was instrumental in growing FWL's Mother Daughter Tea from a small league event to a sold out community event with 750 guests and raising $50,000 for a local park specifically designed for children with special needs.

Lisa also founded and served as President at Give Back Collin County, a resource for other nonprofits to increase their exposure and outreach to volunteers. She loves meeting new people through her networking for volunteer work and her business.

Lisa loves to read, spend time with family and friends, and sing. She's also grateful to Nicole Lynn and the rest of the Wave Makers for giving her this opportunity to write her story.

- Facebook:
  www.Facebook.com/LisaStatzerCoach
  www.Facebook.com/PreDiabeticSupport

- Instagram:
  @LisaStatzer
  @pre_diabetic_support

- LinkedIn
  www.LinkedIn.com/in/LisaStatzer

- Website:
  www.PreDiabeticSupport.com

97559001R00084

Made in the USA
Middletown, DE
05 November 2018